Psychology and Social Sanity • Münsterberg, Hugo

PAGE
Preface 1 vii1
CHAPTER
I. .... 2 Sex Education 2 32
II. .... 15 Socialism 15 7115
III. ....24 The Intellectual Underworld 24 113.. 24
IV. . . 29 Thought Transference 29 14129
V. ....36 The Mind of the Juryman 36 181... 36
VI. 41 Efficiency on the Farm 41 20541
VII. ......45 Social Sins in Advertising 45 229... 45
VIII. ...... 50 The Mind of the Investor 50 253... 50
IX. . .53 Society and the Dance 53 27353
X. .... 56 Naïve Psychology 56 29156

Publisher's Note

Purchase of this book entitles you to a free trial membership in the publisher's book club at www.rarebooksclub.com. (Time limited offer.) Simply enter the barcode number from the back cover onto the membership form on our home page. The book club entitles you to select from millions of books at no additional charge. You can also download a digital copy of this and related books to read on the go. Simply enter the title or subject onto the search form to find them.

Note: This is an historic book. Pages numbers, where present in the text, refer to the first edition of the book and may also be in indexes.

If you have any questions, could you please be so kind as to consult our Frequently Asked Questions page at www.rarebooksclub.com/faqs.cfm? You are also welcome to contact us there.

Publisher: General Books LLC™, Memphis, TN, USA, 2012. ISBN: 9781153786973.
Proofreading: pgdp.net

❧ ❧ ❧ ❧ ❧ ❧ ❧ ❧

PSYCHOLOGY AND SOCIAL SANITY

BY
HUGO MÜNSTERBERG
DOUBLEDAY, PAGE & CO.
GARDEN CITY NEW YORK
1914
Copyright, 1914, by
Doubleday, Page & Company
All rights reserved, including that of translation into foreign languages, including the Scandinavian
To
DR. I. ADLER
IN FRIENDSHIP

PREFACE [vii]

It has always seemed to me a particular duty of the psychologist from time to time to leave his laboratory and with his little contribution to serve the outside interests of the community. Our practical life is filled with psychological problems which have to be solved somehow, and if everything is left to commonsense and to unscientific fancies about the mind, confusion must result, and the psychologist who stands aloof will be to blame.

Hence I tried in my little book "On the Witness Stand" to discuss for those interested in law the value of exact psychology for the problems of the courtroom. In "Psychotherapy" I showed the bearing of a scientific study of the mind on medicine. In "Psychology and the Teacher" I outlined its consequences for educational problems. In "Psychology and Industrial Efficiency" I studied the importance of exact psychology for commerce and industry. And I continue this series by the present little volume, which speaks of psychology's possible service to social sanity. [viii] I cannot promise that even this will be the last, as I have not yet touched on psychology's relation to religion, to art, and to politics.

The field which I have approached this time demanded a different kind of treatment from that in the earlier books. There I had aimed at a certain systematic completeness. When we come to the social questions, such a method would be misleading, as any systematic study of these psychological factors is still a hope for the future. Many parts of the field have never yet been touched by the plow of the psychologist. The only method which seems possible to-day is to select a few characteristic topics of social discussion and to outline for each of them in what sense a psychologist might contribute to the solution or might at least further the analysis of the problem. The aim is to show that our social difficulties are ultimately dependent upon mental conditions which ought to be cleared up with the methods of modern psychology.

I selected as illustrations those social questions which seemed to me most significant for our period. A few of them admitted an approach with experimental methods, others merely a dissection of the psychological and psychophysiological roots. The problems of sex, of socialism, and of superstition seemed to me especially [ix] important, and if some may blame me for overlooking the problem of suffrage, I can at least refer to the chapter on the jury, which comes quite near to this militant question.

Most of this material appears here for the first time. The chapter on thought transference, however, was published in shorter form in the *Metropolitan Magazine*, that on the jury, also abbreviated, in the *Century Magazine*, and that on naïve psychology in the *Atlantic Monthly*. The paper on sexual education is an argument, and at the same time an answer in a vivid discussion. Last summer I published in the New York *Times* an article which dealt with the sex problem. It led to vehement attacks from all over the country. The present long paper replies to them fully. I hope sincerely that it will be my last word in the matter. The advocates of sexual talk now have the floor; from now on I shall stick to the one policy in which I firmly believe, the policy of silence.

Hugo Münsterberg.
Cambridge, Mass., January, 1914.

PSYCHOLOGY AND SOCIAL SANITY

I [3]

SEX EDUCATION

The time is not long past when the social question was understood to mean essentially the question of the distribution of profit and wages. The feeling was that everything would be all right in our society, if this great problem of labour and property could be solved rightly. But in recent years the chief meaning of the phrase has shifted. Of all the social questions the predominant, the fundamentally social one, seems nowadays the problem of sex, with all its side issues of social evils and social vice. It is as if society feels instinctively that these problems touch still deeper layers of the social structure. Even the fights about socialism and the whole capitalistic order do not any longer stir the conscience of the community so strongly as the grave concern about the family. All public life is penetrated by sexual discussions, magazines and newspapers are overflooded with considerations of the sexual problem, on the stage one play of sexual reform is pushed off by the [4] next, the pulpit resounds with sermons on sex, sex education enters into the schools, legislatures and courts are drawn into this whirl of sexualized public opinion; the old-fashioned policy of silence has been crushed by a policy of thundering outcry, which is heard in every home and every nursery. This loudness of debate is surely an effect of the horror with which the appalling misery around us is suddenly discovered. All which was hidden by prudery is disclosed in its viciousness, and this outburst of indignation is the result. Yet it would never have swollen to this overwhelming flood if the nation were not convinced that this is the only way to cause a betterment and a new hope. The evil was the result of the silence itself. Free speech and public discussion alone can remove the misery and cleanse the social life. The parents must know, and the teachers must know, and the boys must know, and the girls must know, if the abhorrent ills are ever to be removed.

But there are two elements in the situation which ought to be separated in sober thought. There may be agreement on the one and yet disagreement on the other. It is hardly possible to disagree on the one factor of the situation, the existence of horrid calamities, and of deplorable abuses in the world of sex, evils of [5] which surely the average person knew rather little, and which were systematically hidden from society, and above all, from the youth, by the traditional method of reticence. To recognize these abscesses in the social organism necessarily means for every decent being the sincere and enthusiastic hope of removing them. There cannot be any dissent. It is a holy war, if society fights for clean living, for protection of its children against sexual ruin and treacherous diseases, against white slavery and the poisoning of married life. But while there must be perfect agreement about the moral duty of the social community, there can be the widest disagreement about the right method of carrying on this fight. The popular view of the day is distinctly that as these evils were hidden from sight by the policy of silence, the right method of removing them from the world must be the opposite scheme, the policy of unveiled speech. The overwhelming majority has come to this conclusion as if it were a matter of course. The man on the street, and what is more surprising, the woman in the home, are convinced that, if we disapprove of those evils, we must first of all condemn the silence of our forefathers. They feel as if he who sticks to the belief in silence must necessarily help the enemies of society, and become responsible for the alarming increase [6] of sexual affliction and crime. They refuse to see that on the one side the existing facts and the burning need for their removal, and on the other side the question of the best method and best plan for the fight, are entirely distinct, and that the highest intention for social reform may go together with the deepest conviction that the popular method of the present day is doing incalculable harm, is utterly wrong, and is one of the most dangerous causes of that evil which it hopes to destroy.

The psychologist, I am convinced, must here stand on the unpopular side. To be sure, he is not unaccustomed to such an unfortunate position in the camp of the disfavoured minority. Whenever a great movement sweeps through the civilized world, it generally starts from the recognition of a great social wrong and from the enthusiasm for a thorough change. But these wrongs, whether they have political or social, economic or moral character, are always the products of both physical and psychical causes. The public thinks first of all of the physical ones. There are railroad accidents: therefore improve the physical technique of the signal system; there is drunkenness: therefore remove the whiskey bottle. The psychical element is by no means ignored. Yet it is treated as if mere insight into the [7] cause, mere good will and understanding, are sufficient to take care of the mental factors involved. The social reformers are therefore always discussing the existing miseries, the possibilities of improvements in the world of things, and the necessity of spreading knowledge and enthusiasm. They do not ask the advice of the psychologist, but only his jubilant approval, and they always feel surprised if he has to acknowledge that there seems to him something wrong in the calculation. The psychologist knows that the mental elements cannot be brought under such a simple formula according to which good will and insight are sufficient; he knows that the mental mechanism which is at work there has its own complicated laws, which must be considered with the same care for detail as those technical schemes for improvement. The psychologist is not astonished that though the technical improvements of the railways are increased, yet one serious accident follows another, as long as no one gives attention to the study of the engineer's mind. Nor is he surprised that while the area of prohibition is expanding rapidly, the consumption of beer and whiskey is nevertheless growing still more quickly, as long as the psychology of the drinker is neglected. The trusts and the labour movements, immigration and the race question, the peace movement and a score of [8] other social problems show exactly the same picture—everywhere insight into old evils, everywhere enthusiasm for new goals, everywhere attention to outside factors, and everywhere negligence of those functions of the mind which are independent of the mere will of the individual.

But now since a new great wave of discussion has arisen, and the sexual problem is stirring the nation, the psychologist's faith in the unpopular policy puts him into an especially difficult position. Whenever he brings from his psychological studies arguments which point to the errors in public prejudices, he can present his facts in full array. Nothing hinders him from speaking with earnestness against the follies of hasty and short-sighted methods in every concern of public life, if he has the courage to oppose the fancies of the day. But the fight in favour of the policy of silence is different. If he begins to shout his arguments, he himself breaks that rôle of silence which he recommends. He speaks for a conviction, which demands from him first of all that he shall not speak. The more eagerly he spreads his science, the more he must put himself in the wrong before his own conscience. He is thus thrown into an unavoidable conflict. If he is silent, the cause of his opponents will prosper, and if he objects [9] with full arguments, his adversaries have a perfect right to claim that he himself sets a poor example and that his psychology helps still more to increase that noisy discussion which he denounces as ruinous to the community. But in this contradictory situation the circle must be broken somewhere, and even at the risk of adding to the dangerous tumult which he condemns, the psychologist must break his silence in order to plead for silence. I shall have to go into all the obnoxious detail, for if I yielded to my feeling of disgust, my reticence would not help the cause while all others are shouting. I break silence in order to convince others that if they were silent, too, our common social hopes and wishes would be nearer to actual fulfilment.

But let us acknowledge from the start that we stand before an extremely complicated question, in which no routine formula can do justice to the manifoldness of problems. Most of these discussions are misshaped from the beginning by the effort to deal with the whole social sex problem, while only one or another feature is seriously considered. Now it is white slavery, and now the venereal diseases; now the demands of eugenics, and now the dissipation of boys; now the influence of literature and drama, and now the effect of sexual education in home and school; now the medical [10] situation and the demands of hygiene, and now the moral situation and the demands of religion; now the influence on the feministic movement, and now on art and social life; now the situation in the educated middle classes, and now in the life of the millions. We ought to disentangle the various threads in this confusing social tissue and follow each by itself. We shall see soon enough that not only the various elements of the situation awake very different demands, but that often any single feature may lead to social postulates which interfere with each other. Any regulation prescription falsifies the picture of the true needs of the time.

II

We certainly follow the present trend of the discussion if we single out first of all the care for the girls who are in danger of becoming victims of private or professional misuse as the result of their ignorance of the world of erotics. This type of alarming news most often reaches the imagination of the newspaper reader nowadays, and this is the appeal of the most sensational plays. The spectre of the white slavery danger threatens the whole nation, and the gigantic number of illegitimate births seems fit to shake the most indifferent citizen. Every naïve girl appears a possible victim [11] of man's lust, and all seem to agree that every girl should be acquainted with the treacherous dangers which threaten her chastity. The new programme along this line centres in one remedy: the girls of all classes ought to be informed about the real conditions before they have an opportunity to come into any bodily contact with men. How far the school is to spread this helpful knowledge, how far the wisdom of parents is to fill these blanks of information, how far serious literature is to furnish such science, and how far the stage or even the film is to bring it to the masses, remains a secondary feature of the scheme, however much it is discussed among the social reformers.

The whole new wisdom proceeds according to the simple principle which has proved its value in the field of popular hygiene. The health of the nation has indeed been greatly improved since the alarming ignorance in the matters of prophylaxis in disease has been systematically fought by popular information. If the mosquito or the hookworm or the fly is responsible for diseases from which hundreds of thousands have to suffer, there can be no wiser and straighter policy than to spread this knowledge to every corner of the country. The teachers in the schoolroom and the writers in the popular magazines cannot do better than to repeat the [12] message, until every adult and every child knows where the enemy may be found and helps to destroy the insects and to avoid the dangers of contact. This is the formula after which those reformers want to work who hold the old-fashioned policy of silence in sexual matters to be obsolete. Of course they aim toward a mild beginning. It may start with beautiful descriptions of blossoms and of fruits, of eggs and of hens, before it comes to the account of sexual intercourse and human embryos, but if the talking is to have any effect superior to not talking, the concrete sexual relations must be impressed upon the imagination of the girl before she becomes sixteen years of age.

Here is the real place for the psychological objection. It is not true that you can bring such sexual knowledge into the mind of a girl in the period of her development with the same detachment with which you can deposit in her mind the knowledge about mosquitoes and houseflies. That prophylactic information concerning the influence of the insects on diseases remains an isolated group of ideas, which has no other influence on the mind than the intended one, the influence of guiding the actions in a reasonable direction. The information about her sexual organs and the effects on the sexual organism of men may also have as one of its results a [13] certain theoretical willingness to avoid social dangers. But the far stronger immediate effect is the psychophysiological reverberation in the whole youthful organism with strong reactions on its blood vessels and on its nerves. The individual differences are extremely great here. On every social level we find cool natures whose frigidity would inhibit strong influences in these organic directions. But they are the girls who have least to fear anyhow. With a much larger number the information, however slowly and tactfully imparted, must mean a breaking down of inhibitions which held sexual feelings and sexual curiosity in check.

The new ideas become the centre of attention, the whole world begins to appear in a new light, everything which was harmless becomes full of meaning and suggestion, new problems awake, and the new ideas irradiate over the whole mental mechanism. The new problems again demand their answers. Just the type of girl to whom the lure might become dangerous will be pushed to ever new inquiries, and if the policy of information is accepted in principle, it would be only wise to furnish her with all the supplementary knowledge which covers the multitude of sexual perversions and social malpractices of which to-day many a clean married woman has not the faintest idea. But to such a [14] girl who knows all, the surroundings appear in the new glamour. She understands now how her body is the object of desire, she learns to feel her power, and all this works backward on her sexual irritation, which soon overaccentuates everything which stands in relation to sex. Soon she lives in an atmosphere of high sexual tension in which the sound and healthy interests of a young life have to suffer by the hysterical emphasis on sexuality. The Freudian psychoanalysis, which threatens to become the fad of the American neurologists, probably goes too far when it seeks the cause for all neurasthenic and hysteric disturbances in repressed sexual ideas of youth. But no psychotherapist can doubt that the havoc which secret sexual thoughts may bring to the neural life, especially of the unbalanced, is tremendous. Broken health and a distorted view of the social world with an unsound, unclean, and ultimately immoral emphasis on the sexual relations may thus be the sad result for millions of girls, whose girlhood under the policy of the past would have remained untainted by the sordid ideas of man as an animal.

Yet the calamity would not be so threatening if the effect of sexual instruction were really confined to the putrid influence on the young imagination. The real outcome is not only such a revolution in the thoughts, [15] but the power which it gains over action. We have only to consider the mechanism which nature has provided. The sexual desire belongs to the same group of human instincts as the desire for food or the desire for sleep, all of which aim toward a certain biological end, which must be fulfilled in order to secure life. The desire for food and sleep serves the individual himself, the desire for the sexual act serves the race. In every one of these cases nature has furnished the body with a wonderful psychophysical mechanism which enforces the outcome automatically. In every case we have a kind of circulatory process into which mental excitements and physiological changes enter, and these are so subtly related to each other that one always increases the other, until the maximum desire is reached, to which the will must surrender. Nature needs this automatic function; otherwise the vital needs of individual and race might be suppressed by other interests, and neglected. In the case of the sexual instinct, the mutual relations between the various parts of this circulatory process are especially complicated. Here it must be sufficient to say that the idea of sexual processes produces dilation of blood vessels in the sexual sphere, and that this physiological change itself becomes the source and stimulus for more vivid sexual feelings, [16] which associate themselves with more complex sexual thoughts. These in their turn reinforce again the physiological effect on the sexual organ, and so the play goes on until the irritation of the whole sexual apparatus and the corresponding sexual mental emotions reach a height at which the desire for satisfaction becomes stronger than any ordinary motives of sober reason.

This is the great trick of nature in its incessant service to the conservation of the animal race. Monogamic civilization strives to regulate and organize these race instincts and to raise culture above the mere lure of nature. But that surely cannot be done by merely ignoring that automatic mechanism of nature. On the contrary, the first demand of civilization must be to make use of this inborn psychophysical apparatus for its own ideal human purposes, and to adjust the social behaviour most delicately to the unchangeable mechanism. The first demand, accordingly, ought to be that we excite no one of these mutually reinforcing parts of the system, neither the organs nor the thoughts nor the feelings, as each one would heighten the activities of the others, and would thus become the starting point of an irrepressible demand for sexual satisfaction. The average boy or girl cannot give theoretical attention to the thoughts concerning sexuality without [17] the whole mechanism for reinforcement automatically entering into action. We may instruct with the best intention to suppress, and yet our instruction itself must become a source of stimulation, which necessarily creates the desire for improper conduct. The policy of silence showed an instinctive understanding of this fundamental situation. Even if that traditional policy had had no positive purpose, its negative function, its leaving at rest the explosive sexual system of the youth, must be acknowledged as one of those wonderful instinctive procedures by which society protects itself.

The reformer might object that he gives not only information, but depicts the dangers and warns against the ruinous effects. He evidently fancies that such a black frame around the luring picture will be a strong enough countermotive to suppress the sensual desire. But while the faint normal longing can well be balanced by the trained respect for the mysterious unknown, the strongly accentuated craving of the girl who knows may ill be balanced by any thought of possible disagreeable consequences. Still more important, however, is a second aspect. The girl to whom the world sex is the great taboo is really held back from lascivious life by an instinctive respect and anxiety. As soon as girl and boy are knowers, all becomes a matter [18] of naked calculation. What they have learned from their instruction in home and school and literature and drama is that the unmarried woman must avoid becoming a mother. Far from enforcing a less sensuous life, this only teaches them to avoid the social opprobrium by going skilfully to work. The old-fashioned morality sermon kept the youth on the paths of clean life; the new-fashioned sexual instruction stimulates not only their sensual longings, but also makes it entirely clear to the young that they have nothing whatever to fear if they yield to their voluptuousness but make careful use of their new physiological knowledge. From my psychotherapeutic activity, I know too well how much vileness and perversity are gently covered by the term flirtation nowadays in the circle of those who have learned early to conceal the traces. The French type of the demi-vierge is just beginning to play its rôle in the new world. The new policy will bring in the great day for her, and with it a moral poisoning which must be felt in the whole social atmosphere.

III

We have not as yet stopped to examine whether at least the propaganda for the girl's sexual education starts rightly when it takes for granted that ignorance [19] is the chief source for the fall of women. The sociological student cannot possibly admit this as a silent presupposition. In many a pathetic confession we have read as to the past of fallen girls that they were not aware of the consequences. But it would be utterly arbitrary to construe even such statements as proofs that they were unaware of the limits which society demanded from them. If a man breaks into a neighbour's garden by night to steal, he may have been ignorant of the fact that shooting traps were laid there for thieves, but that does not make him worthy of the pity which we may offer to him who suffers by ignorance only. The melodramatic idea that a straightforward girl with honest intent is abducted by strangers and held by physical force in places of degradation can simply be dismissed from a discussion of the general situation. The chances that any decent man or woman will be killed by a burglar are a hundred times larger than that a decent girl without fault of her own will become the victim of a white slavery system which depends upon physical force. Since the new policy of antisilence has filled the newspapers with the most filthy gossip about such imaginary horrors, it is not surprising that frivolous girls who elope with their lovers later invent stories of criminal detention, first by half [20] poisoning and afterward by handcuffing. Of all the systematic, thorough investigations, that of the Vice Commission of Philadelphia seems so far the most instructive and most helpful. It shows the picture of a shameful and scandalous social situation, and yet, in spite of years of most insistent search by the best specialists, it says in plain words that "no instances of actual physical slavery have been specifically brought to our attention."

This does not contradict in the least the indubitable fact that in all large cities white slavery exists in the wider sense of the word—that is, that many girls are kept in a life of shame because the escape from it is purposely made difficult to them. They are held constantly in debt and are made to believe that their immunity from arrest depends upon their keeping on good terms with the owners of disorderly houses. But the decisive point for us is that while they are held back at a time when they know too much, they are not brought there by force at a time when they know too little. The Philadelphia Vice Report analyzes carefully the conditions and motives which have brought the prostitutes to their life of shame. The results of those hundreds of interviews point nowhere to ignorance. The list of reasons for entering upon such a life brings information like this: "She liked [21] the man," "Wanted to see what immoral life was like," "Sneaked out for pleasure, got into bad company," "Would not go to school, frequented picture shows, got into bad company," "Thought she would have a better time," "Envied girls with fine clothes and gay time," "Wanted to go to dances and theatres," "Went with girls who drank, influenced by them," "Liked to go to moving picture shows," "Did not care what happened when forbidden to marry." With these personal reasons go the economic ones: "Heard immorality was an easy way to make money, which she needed," "Decided that this was the easiest way of earning money," "Wanted pretty clothes," "Never liked hard work," "Tired of drudgery at home," "Could make more money this way than in a factory." Only once is it reported: "Chloroformed at a party, taken to man's house and ruined by him." If that is true, we have there simply a case of actual crime, against which nobody can be protected by mere knowledge. In short, a thorough study indicates clearly that the girl who falls is not pushed passively into her misery.

Surely it is alarming to read that last year in one single large city of the Middle West two hundred school girls have become mothers, but whoever studies the real sociological material cannot doubt that every one [22] of those two hundred knew very clearly that she was doing something which she ought not to do. Every one of them had knowledge enough, and if the knowledge was often vague and dirty, the effect would not have been improved by substituting for it more knowledge, even if it were clearer and scientifically more correct. What every one of those two hundred girls needed was less knowledge—that is, less familiarity of the mind with this whole group of erotic ideas, and through this a greater respect for and fear of the unknown. Nobody who really understands the facts of the sexual world with the insight of the physician will deny that nevertheless treacherous dangers and sources of misfortune may be near to any girl, and that they might be avoided if she knew the truth. But then it is no longer a question of a general truth, which can be implanted by any education, but a specific truth concerning the special man. The husband whom she marries may be a scoundrel who infects her with ruinous disease, but even if she had read all the medical books beforehand it would not have helped her.

IV

The situation of the boys seems in many respects different. They are on the aggressive side. There is [23] no danger that by their lack of knowledge they will be lured into a life of humiliation, but the danger of their ruin is more imminent and the risk which parents run with them is far worse. Any hour of reckless fun may bring them a life of cruel suffering. The havoc which venereal diseases bring to the men of all social classes is tremendous. The Report of the Surgeon-General of the Army for 1911 states that with the mean strength of about seventy-three thousand men in the army, the admissions to the hospitals on account of venereal diseases were over thirteen thousand. That is, of any hundred men at least eighteen were ill from sexual infection. The New York County Hospital Society reports two hundred and forty-three thousand cases of venereal disease treated in one year, as compared with forty-one thousand five hundred and eighty-five cases of all other communicable diseases. This horrible sapping of the physical energies of the nation, with the devastating results in the family, with the poisoning of the germs for the next generation, and with the disastrous diseases of brain and spinal cord, is surely the gravest material danger which exists. How small compared with that the thousands of deaths from crime and accidents and wrecks! how insignificant the harvest of human life which any war may reap! And all this can [24] ultimately be avoided, not only by abstinence, but by strict hygiene and rigorous social reorganization. At this moment we have only to ask how much of a change for the better can be expected from a mere sexual education of the boys.

From a psychological point of view, this situation appears much more difficult than that of the girls. All psychological motives speak for a policy of silence in the girls' cases. For the boys, on the other hand, the importance of some hygienic instruction cannot be denied. A knowledge of the disastrous consequences of sexual diseases must have a certain influence for good, and the grave difficulty lies only in the fact that nevertheless all the arguments which speak against the sexual education of the girls hold for the boys, too. The harm to the youthful imagination, the starting of erotic thoughts with sensual excitement in consequence of any kind of sexual instruction must be still greater for the young man than for the young woman, as he is more easily able to satisfy his desires. We must thus undoubtedly expect most evil consequences from the instruction of the boys; and yet we cannot deny the possible advantages. Their hygienic consciousness may be enriched and their moral consciousness tainted by the same hour of well-meant instruction. With the girls an [25] energetic no is the only sane answer; with the boys the social reformer may well hesitate between the no and the yes. The balance between fear and hope may be very even there. Yet, however depressing such a decision may be, the psychologist must acknowledge that even here the loss by frank discussion is greater than the gain.

A serious warning lies in the well-known fact that of all professional students, the young medical men have the worst reputation for their reckless indulgence in an erotic life. They know most, and it is psychologically not surprising that just on that account they are most reckless. The instinctive fear of the half knower has left them; they live in an illusory safety, the danger has become familiar to them, and they deceive themselves with the idea that the particular case is harmless. If the steps to be taken were to be worked out at the writing desk in cool mood and sober deliberation, the knowledge would at least often be a certain help, but when the passionate desire has taken hold of the mind and the organic tension of the irritated body works on the mind, there is no longer a fair fight with those sober reasons. The action of the glands controls the psychophysical reactions, so that the ideas which would lead to opposite response are inhibited. Alcohol and the imitative mood of social gayety may help to dull those hygienic [26] fears, but on the whole the mere sexual longing is sufficient to break down the reminiscence of medical warning. The situation for the boy is then ultimately this: A full knowledge of the chances of disease will start in hours of sexual coolness on the one side a certain resolution to abstain from sexual intercourse, and on the other side a certain intention to use protective means for the prevention of venereal diseases. As soon as the sexual desire awakes, the decision of the first kind will become the less effective, and will be the more easily overrun the more firmly the idea is fixed that such preventive means are at his disposal. At the same time the discussion of all these sexual matters, even with their gruesome background, will force on the mind a stronger engagement with sexual thought than had ever before occurred, and this will find its discharge in an increased sexual tension. On the other hand, this new knowledge of means of safety will greatly increase the playing with danger. Of course it may be said that the education ought not to refer only to sexual hygiene, but that it ought to be a moral education. That, however, is an entirely different story. We shall speak about it; we shall put our faith in it, but at present we are talking of that specific sexual education which is the fad of the day. [27]

V

Sexual education, to be sure, does not necessarily mean education of young people only. The adults who know, the married men and women of the community, may not know enough to protect their sons and daughters. And the need for their full information may stretch far beyond their personal family interests. They are to form the public opinion which must stand behind every real reform, their consciences must be stirred, the hidden misery must be brought before them. Thus they need sexual education as much as the youngsters, only they need it in a form which appeals to them and makes them willing to listen; and our reformers have at last discovered the form. The public must be taught from the stage of the theatre. The magazine with its short stories on sex incidents, the newspaper with its sensational court reports, may help to carry the gruesome information to the masses, but the deepest impression will always be made when actual human beings are shown on the stage in their appealing distress, as living accusations against the rotten foundations of society. The stage is overcrowded with sexual drama and the social community inundated with discussions about it.

It is not easy to find the right attitude toward this [28] red-light literature. Many different interests are concerned, and it is often extremely difficult to disentangle them. Three such interests stand out very clearly: the true æsthetic one, the purely commercial one, and the sociological one. It would be wonderful if the æsthetic culture of our community had reached a development at which the æsthetic attitude toward a play would be absolutely controlling. If we could trust this æsthetic instinct, no other question would be admissible but the one whether the play is a good work of art or not. The social inquiry whether the human fates which the poet shows us suggests legislative reforms or hygienic improvements would be entirely inhibited in the truly artistic consciousness. It would make no difference to the spectator whether the action played in Chicago or Petersburg, whether it dealt with men and women of to-day or of two thousand years ago. The human element would absorb our interest, and as far as the joys and the miseries of sexual life entered into the drama, they would be accepted as a social background, just as the landscape is the natural background. A community which is æsthetically mature enough to appreciate Ibsen does not leave "The Ghosts" with eugenic reform ideas. The inherited paralysis on a luetic basis is accepted there as a tragic element of human fate. On [29] the height of true art the question of decency or indecency has disappeared, too. The nude marble statue is an inspiration, and not a possible stimulus to frivolous sensuality, if the mind is æsthetically cultivated. The nakedness of erotic passion in the drama of high æsthetic intent before a truly educated audience has not the slightest similarity to the half-draped chorus of sensual operetta before a gallery which wants to be tickled. But who would claim that the dramatic literature of the sexual problems with which the last seasons have filled the theatres from the orchestra to the second balcony has that sublime æsthetic intent, or that it was brought to a public which even posed in an æsthetic attitude! As far as any high aim was involved, it was the antiæsthetic moral value. The plays presented themselves as appeals to the social conscience, and yet this idealistic interpretation would falsify the true motives on both sides. The crowd went because it found the satisfaction of sexual curiosity and erotic tension through the unveiled discussion of social perversities. And the managers produced the plays because the lurid subjects with their appeal to the low instincts, and therefore with their sure commercial success, could here escape the condemnation of police and decent public as they were covered by the pretence [30] of social reform. How far the writers of the play of prostitution prostituted art in order to share the commercial profits in this wave of sexual reform may better remain undiscussed.

What do these plays really teach us? I think I have seen almost all of them, and the composite picture in my mind is one of an absurdly distorted, exaggerated, and misleading view of actual social surroundings, suggesting wrong problems, wrong complaints, and wrong remedies. When I studied the reports of the vice commissions of the large American and European cities, the combined image in my consciousness was surely a stirring and alarming one, but it had no similarity with the character of those melodramatic vagaries. Even the best and most famous of these fabrications throw wrong sidelights on the social problems, and by a false emphasis inhibit the feeling for the proportions of life. If in "The Fight" the father, a senator, visits a disorderly house, unlocks the room in which the freshest fruit is promised him, and finds there his young daughter who has just been abducted by force, the facts themselves are just as absurd as the following scenes, in which this father shows that the little episode did not make the slightest impression on him. He coolly continues to fight against those politicians who want to [31] remove such places from the town. In "Bought and Paid For" marriage itself is presented as white slavery. The woman has to tolerate the caresses of her husband, even when he has drunk more champagne than is wise for him. The play makes us believe that she must suffer his love because she was poor before she married and he has paid her with a life of luxury. Where are we to end if such logic in questions of sexual intercourse is to benumb common sense? England brought us "The Blindness of Virtue," the story of a boy and a girl whom we are to believe to be constantly in grave danger because they are ignorant, while in reality nothing happens, and everything suggests that the moral danger for this particular girl would have been much greater if she had known how to enjoy love without consequences.

The most sensational specimen of the group was "The Lure." It would be absurd to face this production from any æsthetic point of view. It would be unthinkable that a work of such crudeness could satisfy a metropolitan public, even if some of the most marked faults of construction were acknowledged as the results of the forceful expurgation of the police. Nevertheless, the only significance of the play lies outside of its artistic sphere, and belongs entirely to its effort to help [32] in this great social reform. The only strong applause, which probably repeats itself every evening, broke out when the old, good-natured physician said that as soon as women have the vote the white slavers will be sent to the electric chair. But it is worth while to examine the sermon which a play of this type really preaches, and to become aware of the illusions with which the thoughtless public receives this message. All which we see there on the stage is taken by the masses as a remonstrance against the old, cowardly policy of silence, and the play is to work as a great proof that complete frankness and clear insight can help the daughters of the community.

The whole play contains the sad story of two girls. There is Nell. What happened to her? She is the daughter of a respectable banker in a small town. A scoundrel, a commercial white slaver, a typical Broadway "cadet" with luring manners, goes to the small town, finds access to the church parlours, is introduced to the girl, and after some courtship he elopes with her and makes her believe that they are correctly married. After the fraudulent marriage with a falsified license he brings her into a metropolitan disorderly house and holds her there by force. Of course this is brutal stage exaggeration, but even if this impossibility were true, [33] what conclusion are we to draw, and what advice are we to give? Does it mean that in future a young girl who meets a nice chap in the church socials of her native town ought to keep away from him, because she ought all the time to think that he might be a delegate of a Broadway brothel? To fill a girl with suspicions in a case like that of Nell would be no wiser than to tell the ordinary man that he ought not to deposit his earnings in any bank, because the cashier might run away with it. To be sure, it would have been better if Nell had not eloped, but is there any knowledge of sexual questions which would have helped her to a wiser decision? On the contrary, she said she did elope because her life in the small town was so uninteresting, and she felt so lonely and was longing for the life of love. She knew all which was to be known then, and if there had been any power to hold her back from the foolish elopement it could have been only a kind of instinctive respect for the traditional demands of society, that kind of respect which grows up from the policy of silence and is trampled to the ground by the policy of loud talk.

The other girl in the play is Sylvia. Her fate is very different. She needs melodramatic money for her sick mother. Her earnings in the department store are not enough. The sly owner of a treacherous employment [34] agency has given her a card over the counter, advising her to come there, when she needs extra employment. The agency keeps open in the evening. She tells her mother that she will seek some extra work there. The mother warns her that there are so many traps for decent girls, and she answers that she is not afraid and that she will be on the lookout. She goes there, and the skilful owner of the agency shows her how miserable the pay would be for any decent evening work, and how easily she can earn all the money she needs for her mother if she is willing to be paid by men. At first she refuses with pathos, but under the suggestive pressure of luring arguments she slowly weakens, and finally consents to exchange her street gown for a fantastic costume of half-nakedness. The feelings of the audience are saved by the detective who breaks in at the decisive moment, but the arguments of the advocates of sexual education cannot possibly be saved after that voluntary yielding. Sylvia knows what she has to expect, and no more intense perusal of literature on the subject of prostitution would have changed her mind. What else in the world could have helped her in such an hour but a still stronger feeling of instinctive repugnance? If Sylvia was actually to put her fate on a mere calculation, with a full knowledge of all the sociological facts [35] involved, she probably reasoned wrongly in dealing with this particular employment agency, but was on the whole not so wrong in deciding that a frivolous life would be the most reasonable way out of her financial difficulties, as her sexual education would include, of course, a sufficient knowledge of all which is needed to avoid conception and infection. She would therefore know that after a little while of serving the lust of men she would be just as intact and just as attractive. If society has the wish to force Sylvia to a decision in the opposite direction, only one way is open: to make the belief in the sacred value of virtue so deep and powerful that any mere reasoning and calculation loses its strength. But that is possible only through an education which relies on the instinctive respect and mystical belief. Only a policy of silence could have saved Sylvia, because that alone would have implanted in her mind an ineffable idea of unknown horrors which would await her when she broke the sacred ring of chastity.

The climax of public discussions was reached when America had its season of Brieux' "Damaged Goods." Its topic is entirely different, as it deals exclusively with the spreading of contagious diseases and the prevention of their destructive influence on the family. Yet the doubt whether such a dramatized medical lesson belongs [36] on the metropolitan stage has here exactly the same justification. Nevertheless, it brings its new set of issues. Brieux' play does not deserve any interest as a drama. With complete sincerity the theatre programme announces, "The object of this play is a study of the disease of syphilis in its bearing on marriage." The play was first produced in Paris in the year 1901. It began its great medical teaching in America in the spring of

1913. Even those who have only superficial contact with medicine know that the twelve years which lie between those dates have seen the greatest progress in the study of syphilis which has ever been made. It is sufficient to think of the Wassermann test, the Ehrlich treatment, the new discoveries concerning the relations of lues and brain disease, and many other details in order to understand that a clinical lesson about this disease written in the first year of the century must be utterly antiquated in its fourteenth year. We might just as well teach the fighting of tuberculosis with the clinical textbook of thirty years ago.

How misleading many of the claims of the play are ought to have struck even the unscientific audience. The real centre of the so-called drama is that the father and the grandmother of the diseased infant are willing to risk the health of the wet nurse rather than to allow [37] the child to go over to artificial feeding. The whole play loses its chief point and its greatest pathetic speech if we do not accept the Parisian view that a sickly child must die if it has its milk from the bottle. The Boston audience wildly applauded the great speech of the grandmother who wants to poison the nurse rather than to sacrifice her grandchild to the drinking of sterilized milk, and yet it was an audience which surely was brought up on the bottle. It would be very easy to write another play in which quite different medical views are presented, and where will it lead us if the various treatments of tuberculosis, perhaps by the Friedmann cures, or of diphtheria, perhaps by chiropractice or osteopathy, are to be fought out on the stage until finally the editors of *Life* would write a play around their usual thesis that the physicians are destroying mankind and that our modern medicine is humbug. As long as the drama shows us human elements, every one can be a party and can take a stand for the motives of his heart. But if the stage presents arguments on scientific questions in which no public is able to examine the facts, the way is open for any one-sided propaganda.

Moreover, what, after all, are the lessons which the men are to learn from these three hours of talk on syphilis? [38] To be sure, it is suggested that it would be best if every young man were to marry early and remain faithful to his wife and take care that she remain faithful to him. But this aphorism will make very little impression on the kind of listener whose tendency would naturally turn him in other directions. He hears in the play far more facts which encourage him in his selfish instincts. He hears the old doctor assuring his patient that not more than a negligible 10 per cent. of all men enter married life without having had sexual intercourse with women. He hears that the disease can be easily cured, that he may marry quite safely after three years, that the harm done to the child can be removed, and that no one ought to be blamed for acquiring the disease, as anybody may acquire it and that it is only a matter of good or bad luck. The president of the Medical Society in Boston drew the perfectly correct consequences when in a warm recommendation of the play he emphasized the importance of the knowledge about the disease, inasmuch as any one may acquire it in a hundred ways which have nothing to do with sexual life. He says anybody may get syphilis by wetting a lead pencil with his lips or from an infected towel or from a pipe or from a drinking glass or from a cigarette. This is medically entirely correct, and yet if Brieux had [39] added this medical truth to all the other medical sayings of his doctor, he would have taken away the whole meaning of the play and would have put it just on the level of a dramatized story about scarlet fever or typhoid.

Yet here, too, the fundamental mistake remains the psychological one. The play hopes to reform by the appeal to fear, while the whole mental mechanism of man is so arranged that in the emotional tension of the sexual desire the argument of the fear that we may have bad luck will always be outbalanced by the hope and conviction that we will not be the one who draws the black ball. And together with this psychological fact goes the other stubborn feature of the mind, which no sermon can remove, that the focussing of the attention on the sexual problems, even in their repelling form, starts too often a reaction of glands and with it sexual thoughts which ultimately lead to a desire for satisfaction.

The cleverest of this group of plays strictly intended for sexual education—as Shaw's "Mrs. Warren's Profession" or plays of Pinero and similar ones would belong only indirectly in this circle—is probably Wedekind's "Spring's Awakening." It brought to Germany, and especially to Berlin, any education which [40] the Friedrichstrasse had failed to bring. To prohibit it would have meant the reactionary crushing of a distinctly literary work by a brilliant writer; to allow it meant to fill the Berlin life for seasons with a new spirit which showed its effects. The sexual discussion became the favourite topic; the girls learned to look out for their safety: and it was probably only a chance that at the same time a wave of immorality overflooded the youth of Berlin. The times of naïve flirtation were over; any indecency seemed allowable if only conception was artificially prevented. The social life of Berlin from the fashionable quarters of Berlin West to the factory quarters of Berlin East was never more rotten and more perverse than in those years in which sexual education from the stage indulged in its orgies.

The central problem is not whether the facts are distorted or not, and whether the suggestions are wise or not, and whether the remedies are practicable or not. All this is secondary to the fundamental question of whether it is wise to spread out such problems before the miscellaneous public of our theatres. No doubt a few of the social reformers are sprinkled over the audiences. There are a few in the boxes as well as in the galleries who discern the realities and who hear the true appeal, even through those grotesque melodramas. [41] But with the overwhelming majority it is quite different. For them it is entertainment, and as such it is devastating. It is quite true that many a piquant comic opera shows more actual frivolity, and no one will underestimate the shady influence of such voluptuous vulgarities in their multicoloured stage setting. Yet from a psychological point of view the effect of the pathetic treatment is far more dangerous than that of the frivolous. A good many well-meaning reformers do not see that, because they know too little of the deeper layers of the sexual imagination. The intimate connection between sexuality and cruelty, perversion and viciousness, may produce much more injurious results in the mind of the average man when he sees the tragedy of the white slave than when he laughs at the farce of the chorus girl. Moreover, even the information which such plays divulge may stimulate some model citizens to help the police and the doctors, but it may suggest to a much larger number hitherto unknown paths of viciousness. The average New Yorker would hear with surprise from the Rockefeller Report on Commercialized Prostitution in New York City that the commission has visited in Manhattan a hundred and forty parlour houses, twenty of which were known to the trade as fifty-cent houses, eighty as one-dollar [42] houses, six as two-dollar houses, and thirty-four as five- and ten-dollar houses. Yet the chances are great that essentially persons with serious interests in social hygiene turn to such books of sober study. But to cry out such information to those Broadway crowds which seek a few hours' fun before they go to the next lobster palace or to the nearest cabaret cannot possibly serve social hygiene.

Worst of all, the theatre, more than any other source of so-called information, has been responsible for the breakdown of the barriers of social reserve in sexual discussions, and that means ultimately in erotic behaviour. The book which the individual man or woman reads at his fireside has no socializing influence, but the play which they see together is naturally discussed, views are exchanged, and all which in old-fashioned times was avoided, even in serious discussion, becomes daily more a matter of the most superficial gossip. When recently at a dinner party a charming young woman whom I had hardly met before asked me, when we were at the oysters, how prostitution is regulated in Germany, and did not conclude the subject before we had reached the ice cream, I saw the natural consequences of this new era of theatre influence. Society, which with the excuse of philanthropic sociology [43] favours erotically tainted problems, must sink down to a community in which the sexual relations become chaotic and turbulent. Finally, the theatre is not open only to the adult. Its filthy message reaches the ears of boys and girls, who, even if they take it solemnly, are forced to think of these facts and to set the whole mechanism of sexual associations and complex reactions into motion. The playwriters know that well, but they have their own theory. When I once remonstrated against the indecencies which are injected into the imagination of the adolescent by the plays, Mr. Bayard Veiller, the talented author of "The Fight," answered in a Sunday newspaper. He said that he could not help thinking of the insane man who objected to throwing a bucket of salt water into the ocean for fear it would turn the ocean salt. "Does not Professor Münsterberg know that you can't put more sex thoughts into the minds of young men and women, because their minds contain nothing else?" If the present movement is not brought to a stop, the time may indeed come when those young minds will not contain anything else. But is that really true of to-day, and, above all, was it true of yesterday, before the curtain was raised on the red-light drama? [44]

VI

How is it possible that with such obvious dangers and such evident injurious effects, this movement on the stage and in literature, in the schools and in the homes, is defended and furthered by so many well-meaning and earnest thinking men and women in the community? A number of causes may have worked together there. It cannot be overlooked that one of the most effective ones was probably the new enthusiasm for the feministic movement. We do not want to discuss here the right and wrong of this worldwide advance toward the fuller liberation of women. If we have to touch on it here, it is only to point out that this connection between the sound elements of the feministic movement and the propaganda for sex education on the new-fashioned lines is really not necessary at all. I do not know whether the feminists are entirely right, but I feel sure that their own principles ought rather to lead them to an opposition to this breaking down of the barriers. It is nothing but a superficiality if they instinctively take their stand on the side of those who spread broadcast the knowledge about sex.

The feminists vehemently object to the dual standard, but if they help everything which makes sex an [45] object of common gossip, it may work indeed toward a uniform standard; only the uniformity will not consist in the men's being chaste like the women, but in the women's being immoral like the men. The feministic enthusiasm turns passionately against those scandalous places of women's humiliation; and yet its chief influence on female education is the effort to give more freedom to the individual girl, and that means to remove her from the authority and discipline of the parental home, to open the door for her to the street, to leave her to her craving for amusement, to smooth the path which leads to ruin. The sincere feminists may say that some of the changes which they hope for are so great that they are ready to pay the price for them and to take in exchange a rapid increase of sexual vice and of erotic disorderliness. But to fancy that the liberation of women and the protection of women can be furthered by the same means is a psychological illusion. The community which opens the playhouses to the lure of the new dramatic art may protect 5 per cent. of those who are in danger to-day, but throws 50 per cent. more into abysses. The feminists who see to the depths of their ideals ought to join full-heartedly the ranks of those who entirely object to this distribution of the infectious germs of sexual knowledge. [46]

Some stray support may come to the new movement also from another side. Some believe that this great emphasis on sexual interests may intensify æsthetic longings in the American commonwealth. No doubt this interrelation exists. No civilization has known a great artistic rise without a certain freedom and joy in sensual life. Prudery always has made true æsthetic unfolding impossible. Yet if we yielded here, we would again be pushed away from our real problem. The æsthetic enthusiast might think it a blessing for the American nation if a great æsthetic outburst were secured, even by the ruin of moral standards: a wonderful blossoming of fascinating flowers from a swampy soil in an atmosphere full of moral miasmas. To be sure, even then it is very doubtful whether any success could be hoped for, as a lightness in sexual matters may be a symptom of an artistic age, but surely is not its cause. The artist may love to drink, but the drink does not make an artist. An æsthetic community may reach its best when it is freed from sexual censorship, but throwing the censor out of the house would not add anything to the æsthetic inspiration of a society which is instinctively indifferent to the artistic calling. Above all, the question for us is not whether the sexual overeducation may have certain pleasant side effects: [47] we ask only how far it succeeds in its intended chief effect of improving morally the social community.

In fact, neither feminism nor æstheticism could have secured this indulgence of the community in the new movement, if one more direct argument had not influenced the conviction of some of our leaders. They reason around one central thought—namely, that the old policy of silence, in which they grew up, has been tried and has shown itself unsuccessful. The horrible dimensions which the social evil has taken, the ruinous effects on family life and national health, are before us. The old policy must therefore be wrong. Let us try with all our might the reform, however disgusting its first appearance may be. This surely is the virile argument of men who know what they are aiming at. And yet it is based on fundamental psychological misapprehensions. It is a great confusion of causes and effects. The misery has this distressing form not on account of the policy of silence, but in spite of it, or rather it took the tremendous dimensions of to-day at the same time that the dam of silence was broken and the flood of sexual gossip rushed in.

We find exactly this relation throughout the history of civilized mankind. To be sure, some editorial writers [48] behave as if the erotic calamity of the day were something unheard of, and as if it demanded a new remedy. The historical retrospect leaves no doubt that periods of sexual tension and of sexual relaxation, of hysteric erotic excitement and of a certain cool indifference have alternated throughout thousands of years. And whenever an age was unusually immoral and lascivious, it was always also a period in which under the mask of scientific interest or social frankness or æsthetic openmindedness the sexual problems were matters of freest discussion. The periods of austerity and restraint, on the other hand, were always characterized also by an unwillingness to talk about sexual relations and to show them in their animal nakedness. Antiquity knew those ups and downs, mediæval times knew them, and in modern centuries the fluctuations have been still more rapid. As soon as a moral age with its policy of silence is succeeded by an immoral age, it is certainly a very easy historical misconstruction to say that the immorality resulted from the preceding conspiracy of silence and that the immorality would disappear if the opposite scheme of frankest speech were adopted. But the fact that this argument is accepted and that the overwhelming majority hails the new régime with enthusiasm is nothing [49] but an almost essential part of the new period, which has succeeded the time of modesty.

Sexual discussion and sexual immorality have always been parts of one circle; sexual silence and moral restraint form another circle. The change from one to the other has come in the history of mankind, usually through new conditions of life, and the primary factor has not been any policy of keeping quiet in respect or of gossiping in curiosity, but the starting point has generally been a change in the life habits. When new wealth has come to a people with new liberties and new desires for enjoyment, the great periods of sexual frivolity have started and brought secondarily the discussions of sex problems, which intensified the immoral life. On the other hand, when a nation in the richness of its life has been brought before new great responsibilities, great social earthquakes and revolutions, great wars for national honour, or great new intellectual or religious ideals, then the sexual tension has been released, the attention has been withdrawn from the frivolous concerns, and the people have settled down soberly to a life of modesty and morality, which brought with it as a natural consequence the policy of reverence and silence. The new situation in America, and to a certain degree all over the world, has come in, too, not [50] through the silence of the preceding generation, but by the sudden change from agricultural to industrial life, with its gigantic cumulation of capital, with its widespread new wealth, with its new ideas of social liberty, with its fading religion, with its technical wonders of luxury and comfort. This new age, which takes its orders from Broadway with its cabarets and tango dances, must ridicule the silence of our fathers and denounce it as a conspiracy. It needs the sexual discussions, as it craves the lurid music and the sensual dances, until finally even the most earnest energies, those of social reform and of hygiene, of intellectual culture and of artistic effort, are forced into the service of this antimoral fashion.

Some sober spectators argue that as things have gone to this extent, it might be wise to try the new policy as an experiment, because matters cannot become worse than they are to-day. But those who yield to the new advice so readily ought again to look into the pages of history, or ought at least to study the situation in some other countries before they proclaim that the climax has been reached. It may be true that it would not be possible to transform still more New York hotels into dancing halls, since the innovation of this fashion, which suggests the dancing epidemics of mediæval times, has [51] reached practically every fashionable hostelry. Yet we may be only at the beginning, as in this vicious circle of craving for sensual life and talking about sexual problems the erotic transformation of the whole social behaviour is usually a rapid one. The Rococo age reached many subtleties, which we do not dream of as yet, but to which the conspiracy against silence may boldly push us. Read the memoirs of Casanova, the Italian of the eighteenth century, whose biography gives a vivid picture of a time in which certainly no one was silent on sexual affairs and in which life was essentially a chain of gallant adventures; even the sexual diseases figured as gallant diseases. In the select American circles it is already noticeable that the favourites of rich men get a certain social acknowledgment. The great masses have not reached this stage at present, which is, of course, very familiar in France. But if we proceed in that rapid rhythm with which we have changed in the last ten years, ten years hence we may have substituted the influence of mistresses for the influence of Tammany grafters, and twenty years hence a Madame Pompadour may be dwelling not far from the White House and controlling the fate of the nation with her small hands, as she did for two decades when Louis XV was king. History has sufficiently shown [52] that these are the logical consequences of the sensualization of a rich people, whose mind is filled with sexual problems. Are we to wait, too, until a great revolution or a great war shakes the nation to its depths and hammers new ideas of morality into its conscience? Even our literature might sink still deeper and deeper. If we begin with the sexual problem, it lies in its very nature that that which is interesting to-day is to-morrow stale, and new regions of sexuality must be opened. The fiction of Germany in the last few years shows the whole pathetic decadence which results. The most abstruse perversions, the ugliest degenerations of sexual sinfulness, have become the favourite topics, and the best sellers are books which in the previous age would have been crushed by police and public opinion alike, but which in the present time are excused under scientific and sociological pretences, although they are more corrupt and carry more infection than any diseases against which they warn.

VII

What is to be done? In one point we all agree: Those who are called to do so must bend their utmost energy toward the purification of the outer forms of community life and of the public institutions. Certain [53] eugenic ideas must be carried through relentlessly; above all, the sexual segregation of the feeble-minded, whose progeny fills the houses of disorder and the ranks of the prostitutes. The hospitals must be wide open for every sexual disease, and all discrimination against diseases which may be acquired by sexual intercourse must be utterly given up in order to stamp out this scourge of mankind, as far as possible, with the medical knowledge of our day. Every effort must be made to suppress places through which unclean temptations are influencing the youth. Parents and doctors should speak in the intimacy of private talk earnest words of warning. The fight against police corruption and graft must be relentlessly carried on so as to have the violation of the laws really punished.

Many means may still seem debatable among those who know the social and medical facts. Certainly some of the eugenic postulates go too far. It is, for instance, extremely difficult to say where the limit is to be set for permissible marriages. There may be no doubt that feeble-mindedness ought not to be transmitted to the next generation, but have we really a right to prevent the marriage of epileptics or psychasthenics? Can we be surprised then that others already begin to demand that neurasthenics shall not marry? Even the [54] health certificate at the wedding may give only an illusion of safety, as the health of too many marriages is destroyed by the escapades of the husband, and it may, on the other hand, lead to a narrowing down under the pressure of arbitrary theories, producing a true race suicide. The question whether the healthy man is the only desirable element of the community is one which allows different answers. Much of the greatest work for the world's progress has been created by men with faulty animal constitutions whose parents would never have received permission to marry from a rigorous eugenic board.

But whatever the sociological reasons for hesitation may be, the state legislators and physicians, the police officers and social workers have no right to stop. They must push forward and force the public life into paths of less injurious and less dangerous sexual habits and customs. Their success will depend upon the energy with which they keep themselves independent of the control of those who do not count with realities. The hope that men will become sexually abstinent outside married life is fantastic, and the book of history ought not to have been written in vain. Any counting on this imaginary overcoming of selfish desire for sexual satisfaction decreases the chances of real hygienic [55] reform. It would even be an inexcusable hypocrisy of the medical profession if, with its consent, one group of specialists behave as if sexual abstinence were the bodily ideal, while thousands of no less conscientious physicians in the world, especially those concerned with nervous diseases, feel again and again obliged to advise sexual intercourse for their patients. We know to-day, even much better than ten years ago, how many serious disturbances result from the suppression of normal sexual life. The past has shown, moreover, that when society succeeded in spreading alarm and in decreasing prostitution by fear, the result was such a rapid increase of perversion and nerve-racking self-abuse that after a short while the normal ways were again preferred as the lesser evil.

And the reformers will need a second limitation of their efforts. They cannot hope for success as long as they fancy that reasoning and calculation and sober balancing of dangers and joys, of injuries and advantages, can ever be the decisive factor of progress. They ought not to forget that as soon as this whole problem is brought down to a mere considering of consequences by the individual, their eugenic hopes may be cruelly shaken. However distressing it is to say it frankly, by mere appeal to reason we shall not turn many girls [56] from the way which leads to prostitution, nor many boys from the anticipation of married life. The girl in the factory, who hesitates between the hard work at the machine for the smallest pay, without pleasures, and the easy money of the street, with an abundance of fun, may in the regrettable life of prosaic reality balance the consequences very differently from the moralist. She has discovered that the ideal of virtue is not so highly valued in her circles as in the middle classes. The loss of her virtue is not such a severe hindrance in her life, and even if she yields for a while to earn her extra money in indecent ways, the chances are great that she may remain more attractive to a possible future husband from her set than if she lived the depressing life of grief and deprivation. The probability of her marrying and becoming the mother in a decent family home may be greater than on the straighter path. It is, of course, extremely sad that reality takes such an immoral way, but just here is the field where the reformers ought to keep their eyes wide open, instead of basing their appeals on illusory constructions about social conditions which do not exist. And if the boys begin to reason, their calculations may count on a still greater probability of good outcome, if they indulge in their pleasures. More than that, the fate of certain European countries shows [57] that when it comes to this clear reasoning, the great turn of the selfish man is from the dangerous prostitute to the clean girl or married woman, to the sisters and wives of his friends, and that means the true ruin of home life.

What is the consequence of all? That the fight ought to be given up? Surely not. But that instead of relying on physical conditions, on fear of diseases, on merely eugenic improvements and on clever reasoning, the reform must come from within, must be one of education and morality, must be controlled, not by bacteriology, but by ethics, must find its strength not from horror of skin diseases, but in the reverence for the ideal values of humanity.

VIII

We must not deceive ourselves as to the gravity of the problem. It is not one of the passing questions which are replaced next season by new ones. State laws and interstate laws may and ought to continue to round off some of the sharp edges, institutions and associations may and ought to succeed in diminishing some of the misery, but the central problem of national policy in the treatment of the youth will stay with us until it has been solved rightly; illustrative instruction cannot [58] be such a solution. We must see with open eyes where we are standing. The American nation of to-day is no longer the America of yesterday. The puritanism which certainly was a spirit of restraint has gone and cannot be brought back. The new wealth and power, the influx of sensuous South European and East European elements, the general trend of our age all over the civilized world, with its technical comfort and its inexpensive luxuries, the receding of religion and many more factors, have given a new face to America in the last fifteen years. A desire for the satisfaction of the senses, a longing for amusements, has become predominant in thousandfold shades from the refined to the vulgar. In such self-seeking periods the sexual desire in its masked and its unmasked forms gains steadily in importance and fascination.

America, moreover, is in a particularly difficult situation. This new longing for joy, even with its erotic touch, brings with it many valuable enrichments of every national life, not least among them the spreading of the sense of beauty. But what is needed is a wholesome national self-control by which an antisocial growth of these emotions will be suppressed. Our present-day American life so far lacks these conditions for the truly harmonious organization of the new tendencies. There [59] are many causes for it. The long puritanic past did not allow that slow European training in æsthetic and harmless social enjoyments. Moreover, the widespread wealth, the feeling of democratic equality, the faintness of truly artistic interests in the masses, all reinforce the craving for the mere tickling of the senses, for amusement of the body, for vaudeville on the stage and in life. The sexual element in this wave of enjoyment becomes reinforced by the American position of the woman outside of the family circle. Her contact with men has been multiplied, her right to seek joy in every possible way has become the corollary of her new independence, her position has become more exposed and more dangerous. And in addition to all this, the chief factor, which alone would be sufficient to give to the situation a threatening aspect: American educationalists do not believe in discipline. As long as the community was controlled by the moral influence of puritanism, the lack of training in subordination under social authority and obedient discipline was without danger, while it strengthened the spirit of political liberty. But to-day, in the period of the new antipuritanic life, the lack of discipline in education means an actual threat to the social safety.

In such a situation what can be more fraught with [60] dangers than to abolish the policy of silence and to uphold the policy of talking and talking about sexual matters with those whose minds were still untouched by the lure. It means to fill the atmosphere in which the growing adolescent moves with sultry ideas, it means to distort the view of the social surroundings, it means to stir up the sexual desires and to teach children how to indulge in them without immediate punishment. Just as in a community of graft and corruption the individual soon loses the finer feeling for honesty, and crime flourishes simply because every one knows that nobody expects anything better, so in a community in which sexual problems are the lessons of the youth and the dinner talk of the adult, the feeling of respect for man's deepest emotions fades away. Man and woman lose the instinctive shyness in touching on this sacred ground, and as the organic desires push and push toward it, the youth soon discovers that the barriers to the forbidden ground are removed and that in their place stands a simple signal with a suggestive word of warning against some easily avoided traps.

From a psychological point of view the right policy would be to reduce the external temptations, above all, the opportunities for contact. Coeducation, for instance, was morally without difficulties twenty years [61] ago, but it is unfit in high schools and colleges for the eastern part of the nation in the atmosphere of to-day. Moreover, the æsthetic spirit ought to be educated systematically, and above all, the whole education of the youth ought to be built on discipline; the lesson by which the youth learns to overcome the desire and to inhibit the will is the most essential for the young American of to-morrow. The policy of silence has never meant that a girl should grow up without the consciousness that the field of sexual facts exists in our social world; on the contrary, those feelings of shame and decency which belong to the steady learning of a clean child from the days of the nursery have strongly impressed on the young soul that such regions are real, but that they must not be approached by curiosity or self-seeking wilfulness. This instinct itself brought something of ideal value, of respect and even of reverence into the most trivial life, however often it became ruined by foul companionship. To strengthen this instinctive emotion of mysterious respect, which makes the young mind shrink from brutal intrusion, will remain the wisest policy, as long as we cannot change that automatic mechanism of human nature by which the sexual thought stimulates the sexual organs. The masses are, of course, in favour of the opposite programme, [62] which is in itself only another symptom of the erotic atmosphere into which the new antipuritanic nation has come. That mechanism of the nervous system furnishes them a pleasant excitement when they read and hear the discussions and plays which bristle with sexual instruction. The magazines which, with the best intentions, fight for the new policy, easily find millions of readers; the plays with their erotic overflow and the moral ending are crowded, and mostly by those who hardly need the instruction any longer. A nation which tries to lift its sexual morality by dragging the sexual problems to the street for the inspection of the crowd, without shyness and without shame, and which wilfully makes them objects of gossip and stage entertainment, is doing worse than Munchausen when he tried to lift himself by his scalp. It seems less important that the youth learn the secrets of sexual intercourse than that their teachers and guardians learn the elements of physiological psychology; the sexual sins of the youth start from the educational sins of the elders.

It is easy to say, as the social reformers and the vice commissioners and the sex instructors and many others have repeated in ever new forms, that "all children's questions should be answered truthfully," and to work up the whole sermon to the final trumpet call, "The [63] truth shall make you free." Yet this is entirely useless as long as we have not defined what we mean by freedom, and above all what we mean by truth. If the child enjoys the beautiful softness of the butterfly's coloured wing, it is surely a truth, if we teach him that seen under the microscope in reality there is no softness there, but large ugly bumps and hollows and that the beautiful impression is nothing but an illusion. But is this truth of the microscope the only truth, and is science the only truth, and is there ever only one truth about the concrete facts of reality? Does truth in this sense not simply mean a certain order into which we bring our experience in the service of certain purposes of thought? We may approach the chaos of life experience with different purposes, and led by any one of them we may reach that consistent unity of ideas for the limited outlook which we call truth. The chemist has a right to consider everything in the world as chemical substances, and the mathematician may take the same things as geometric objects. And yet he who seeks a meaning in these things and a value and an inner development may come to another kind of truth. Only a general philosophy of life can ultimately grade and organize those various relative truths and combine them in an all-embracing unity. [64]

No doubt the physician's scientific discoveries and observations are perfectly true. Man is an animal, and anatomical and physiological conditions control his existence, and if we want to understand this animal's life and want to keep it healthy, we have to ask for the truth of the physician. But shame upon him who wants to educate youth toward the view that man as an animal is the true man! If we educate at all, we educate in the service of culture and civilization. All building up of the youthful mind is itself service to human progress. But this human progress is not a mere growth of the animal race. It has its total meaning in the understanding of man as a soul, determined by purposes and ideals. Not the laws of physiology, but the demands of logic, ethics, æsthetics, and religion control the man who makes history and who serves civilization. He who says that the child's questions ought to be answered truthfully means in this connection that lowest truth of all, the truth of physiology, and forgets that when he opens too early the mind of the boy and the girl to this materialistic truth he at the same time closes it, and closes it perhaps forever, to that richer truth in which man is understood as historic being, as agent for the good and true and beautiful and eternal. [65]

Give to the child the truth, but that truth which makes life worth living, that truth which teaches him that life is a task and a duty, and that his true health and soundness and value will depend upon the energy with which he makes the world and his own body with its selfish desires subservient to unselfish ideals. If you mean by the truth that half-truth of man as a sexual creature of flesh and nerves, the child to whom you offer it will be led to ever new questions, and if you go on answering them truthfully as the new fashion suggests, your reservoir will soon be emptied, even if the six volumes of Havelock Ellis' "Psychology of Sex" are fully at your disposal. But the more this species of truth is given out, the more life itself, for which you educate the child, will appear to him unworthy and meaningless. If the truth of civilized life is merely that which natural science can analyze, then life has lost its honour and its loyalty, its enthusiasm and its value. He who sees the truth in the idealistic aspect of man will not necessarily evade the curious question of the child who is puzzled about the naturalistic processes around him. But instead of whetting his appetite for unsavoury knowledge, he will seriously influence the young mind to turn the attention into the opposite direction. He will speak to him about the fact that [66] there is something animal-like in the human being, but will add that the true values of life lie just in overcoming the low instincts in the interest of high aims. He will point to those hidden naturalistic realities as something not overimportant, but as something which a clean boy and girl do not ask about and with which only the imagination of bad companions is engaged. An instinctive indifference and aversion to the contact with anything low and impure can easily be developed in every healthy child amid clean surroundings. Why is the boy to live and to die for the honour of his country? Why is he to devote himself to the search for knowledge? Why is he to fight for the growth of morality? Why does he not confine himself to mere seeking for comfort and ease and satisfaction of the senses? All which really creates civilization and human progress depends upon symbols and belief. As soon as we make all those symbols of the historic community, all the ideals of honour and devotion, righteousness and beauty, glory and faithfulness, mere matters of scientific calculation, they stare us in the face as sheer absurdities; and yet we might again misname that as truth. Then it is the untruth which makes us free, it is the non-scientific, humanistic aspect which liberates us from the slavery of our low desires. [67]

Certainly there will always be some wild boys and girls in the school who try to spread filthy knowledge, but if the atmosphere is filled with respect and reverence, and the minds are trained by inner discipline and morality, the contagion of such mischievous talk will reach only those children who have the disposition of the degenerate. The majority will remain uncontaminated. Plenty of lewd literature in the circulars of the quacks and even in the sensational newspapers will reach their eye and their brain, and yet it will leave not the slightest trace. The trained, clean mind develops a moral antitoxin which at every pulse-beat of life destroys the poisonous toxins produced by the germs which enter the system. The red lanterns will never be entirely extinguished in any large city the world over, but the boy who has developed a sense of respect and reverence and an instinctive desire for moral cleanliness and a power to overcome selfish impulses, will pass them by and forget them when he comes to the next street corner. But the other, whose imagination has been filled with a shameless truth and who receives as his protection merely a warning which appeals to his fear of diseases, may pass that red lantern entrance at first, but at the next block his tainted imagination will have overcome the fear, and with the reckless confidence that [68] he will know how to protect himself and that he will have good luck he, too, like the moth, will feel attracted toward the red light and will turn back. We can prohibit alcohol, but we cannot prohibit the stimulus to sexual lust. It is always present, and the selfish desire, made rampant by a society which craves amusement, will always be stronger than any social argument or any talk of possible individual danger. The only effective check is the deep inner respect, and we must teach it to the youth, or the whole nation will have to be taught it soon by the sterner discipline of history. The genius of mankind cannot be deceived by philistine phrases about the conspiracy of silence. The decision to be silent was a solemn pledge to the historic spirit of human progress, which demands its symbols, its conventions, and its beliefs. To destroy the harvest of these ideal values, because some weeds have grown up [69] with them, by breaking down the dams and allowing the flood of truth-talk to burst in is the great psychological crime of our day. There is only one hope and salvation: let us build up the dam again to protect our field for a better to-morrow. [70]

II [71]

SOCIALISM

The history of socialism has been a history of false prophecies. Socialism started with a sure conviction that under the conditions of modern industry the working class must be driven into worse and worse misery. In reality the development has gone the opposite way. There are endlessly more workingmen with a comfortable income than ever before. The prophets also knew surely that the wealth from manufacturing enterprises would be concentrated with fewer and fewer men, while history has taken the opposite turn and has distributed the shares of the industrial companies into hundreds of thousands of hands. Other prophecies foretold the end of the small farmer, still others the uprooting of the middle class, others gave the date for the great crash; and everything would have come out exactly as the prophets foresaw it, if they had not forgotten to consider many other factors in the social situation which gave to the events a very different turn. But it may be [72] acknowledged that the wrong prophesying was done not only by the socialists, but no less by the spectators. I myself have to confess my guilt. Many years ago when I wrote my German book on "The Americans," I declared with the ringing voice of the prophet that socialism would never take hold of

America. It was so easy to show that its chief principles and fundamental doctrines were directly opposed to the deepest creeds of Americanism and that the whole temper of the population was necessarily averse to the anticapitalistic fancies. The individualistic striving, the faith in rivalry, the fear of centralization, the political liberty, the lack of class barriers which makes it possible for any one to reach the highest economic power, all work against socialism, and all are essential for American democracy. Above all, the whole American life was controlled by the feeling that individual wealth is the measurement of individual success, and even puritanism had an internal affinity to capitalism. Hence socialism could not mean anything but an imported frill which could not be taken seriously by the commonwealth. In later editions of the book I modified my predictions slightly, and to-day I feel almost inclined to withdraw my prophecy entirely.

To be sure, I still think that the deepest meaning of [73] Americanism and of the American mission in the world is farther away from socialism than the spirit of any other nation. And yet—I do not say that I fear, or that I hope, but I believe—socialism has in no other land at present such good chances to become the policy of the state. The country has entered into a career of progressive experiments; the traditional respect for the old constitutional system of checks and balances to the mere will of the crowd has been undermined. The real legislative reign of the masses has just begun and it would seem only natural that such an entirely new movement should be pushed forward by its own momentum. If the genius of America, which was conservative, turns radical, the political machinery here would be more fit than that of any other land to allow the enforcement of socialism. This will not come to-day or to-morrow, but that socialism may suddenly be with us the day after to-morrow is the possibility with which the neutral observer must count. There is no need of directly reversing the prophecies, as there are many energies in the soul of the nation which may react against this new tendency and may automatically check this un-American economic capture. It is a fight with equal chances, and which side will win cannot be foreseen. But if socialism really has entered the [74] realm of practical possibilities, it becomes the duty of everybody to study the new demands from his own standpoint. The nation must see the facts from many angles before it can decide on this tremendous issue. Any one-sidedness, whether in favour of or against the new programme, must be dangerous. In such a situation even the psychologist may be excused for feeling tempted to contribute his little share to the discussion.

The central problem of the psychologist would evidently lie in the question whether the socialistic reformer calculates with right ideas about the human mind. There might, to be sure, be a little psychological side-show not without a peculiar interest at the entrance gate of socialism. We might turn the question, what is the psychology of the socialist, so as to mean, not with what psychology does the socialist operate, but what goes on in the socialist's mind. No doubt the motives have gone through deep changes even in the mind of the cultured leaders. When Karl Marx laid the foundations of socialism, he was moved solely by the desire to recognize a necessary development. It was the interest of the theorist. He showed that the things which the socialist depicted simply had to come. He did not ask whether they are good or bad. They were for him ultimately natural events which were to be forestalled. The [75] leaders to-day see it all in a new light. The socialistic state is to them a goal to the attainment of which all energies ought to be bent. Not their theoretical knowledge, but their practical conscience, leads them to their enthusiasm for a time without capitalism. In the minds of the masses, however, who vote for the socialist here or abroad, the glory of moral righteousness is somewhat clouded by motives less inspiring in quality. The animosity against the men of wealth rushes into the mental foreground, and if it is claimed that the puritans disliked the bear baiting not because it gave pain to the bears, but because it gave pleasure to the onlookers, it sometimes seems as if the socialists, too, desire the change, not in order that the poor gain more comfort, but in order that the rich be punished. And many cleaner motives have mixed in, which resulted from the general change of conditions. The labourer lives to-day in a cultural atmosphere which was unknown to his grandfathers. He reads the same newspaper as his employers, he thinks in the same catch phrases, and has essentially the same foundation of education. Moreover the publicity of our life in this era of print too easily teaches the workingman that his master may be neither better nor wiser than he and his comrades. And finally, the political and economic discussions of the last [76] half century have made it perfectly clear to him that the removing of the material misery lies in the realm of practical possibility, and that even without bombs a new economic order may be created almost as easily as a new tariff law or an income tax or an equal suffrage. Hence it is not surprising that all these motives combined turn the imagination of millions to the new panaceas.

But if low motives are mixed with high ones in the mind of the champions of socialism, they certainly have never stopped assuring us that it is worse with their opponents. Marx himself declared passionately that greed was the deepest spring, that "the most violent and malignant passions of the human breast, the furies of private interest" are whipping men into the battle against socialism. However that may be, the discussions in the clubroom and in the political hall perhaps oftener suggest a less malignant motive, a persistent carelessness, which keep the friends of the capitalistic order from making the effort really to find out at what the socialists are aiming. The largest part of the private and public accusations of socialism starts from the conviction that socialism means that all men must have equal property, and in consideration of the fact that no real socialist demands that, and that the socialists have always insisted that this is not their intention, [77] there indeed seems to be some psychology necessary to understand why the antisocialists do not take the trouble to find out first what socialism is.

But here we are not engaged in the mental analysis of those who fight about socialism. We want rather to ask whether the human minds are rightly understood by those who tell us that socialism is, or is not, the solution of our social problems. And if we turn to this fundamental question whether socialism ought to become the form of our society, the chief thing will be to avoid a mistake in the discussion which pervades the largest part of our present-day literature. The problem is no longer, as it was in the childhood days of socialistic debate, whether the historical necessities must bring socialism. We know that socialism will come, if we like it, and that we can avoid it, if we hate it, and that everything therefore depends upon the decision of the community whether it wants to work for or against the great economic revolution. It is thus not a question of facts, but of preferences, of judgments, of ideals. We do not simply have to exchange wise words as to that which will come anyhow, but we have to make up our mind whether it appears to us desirable or not desirable, and that means, whether it is in harmony with our purpose or not. [78]

But this forces on us as the very first inquiry: what is the purpose of our social economic system to be? Just here the mistake comes into the debates. We hear eloquent orations about the merits or demerits of socialism, without any effort being made to define clearly for what end it is useful or useless. It is meaningless to claim that socialism is good, if we do not know for what it is good, and the whole flippancy of the discussion too often becomes apparent when we stop and inquire what purposes the speaker wants to see fulfilled. We find a wobbling between two very different possible human purposes, with the convenient scheme of exchanging the one for the other, when the defender gets into a tight place. These two great purposes are economic development and human happiness. With the gesture of high cultural inspiration the new scheme is praised to us as a way toward a greater economic achievement by mankind, a fuller development of human economic life. But as soon as doubts are cast on the value of the scheme for this noble purpose, the argument slips into the other groove and shows us that socialism is wonderful for removing human misery and bringing sweet happiness to numberless men, women, and children. According to the same scheme, of course, when we do not feel convinced that socialism will be [79] the remedy for unhappiness, the scene is changed again, and we hear that it will be splendid for economic progress.

No one would claim that the two ends have nothing to do with each other. We might define the progress of economic life in such a way that the increase of human happiness belongs within its compass. Or we might show that widespread human happiness would be an advantageous condition for the development of economic civilization. But in any case the two are not the same, and even their intimate relation may appear artificial. To discuss the value of a new scheme without perfectly clearing up and sharply discriminating the possible ends for which it may be valuable, can never be helpful toward the fundamental solution of a problem. Nobody doubts that human progress is a worthy aim, and no one denies that human happiness is a beautiful goal. Hence we may evade the philosophical duty of proving through reasons that they are justified ends. We take them for granted, and we only insist that the one is not the other, and that it is utterly in vain to measure the value of socialism with reference to these two ideals, as long as we do not cleanly discriminate for which of the two socialism can be valuable. In itself it may very well be that it is splendid [80] for human progress, but unfit for promoting human happiness, or that it is powerless for the development of mankind, but most successful for the increase of human joy.

Hence we ask at first only: how does the old or the new system serve the progress of mankind? What this human progress means is clearly interpreted by the history of five thousand years of civilization. It is the history of the growing differentiation of human demands and fulfilments. Every new stage in the culture of mankind developed new desires and new longings from nature and from society, but it also brought with it new means of satisfying the longings and fulfilling the desires. The two belong most intimately together. The new means of fulfilment stimulate new desires of intellect and emotion and will, and the new desires lead to further means of their satisfaction. Thus there is an incessant automatic enrichment, an endless differentiation, a thousand new needs on the height of civilization where the primitive race found a few elementary demands, and a thousand new schemes of material technique and of social, institutional life where the lower culture found all it needed with simple devices. It is an unfolding not dissimilar to that which the plants and the animals have shown in their organic [81] life in the long periods of natural evolution. The development from the infusors to the monkeys was such a steady increase in the manifoldness of functions. The butterfly is as well adjusted to its life conditions and as well off as the fish, and the fish as well off as the elephant, and in the evolution of economic civilization as in that of the kingdom of animals the advance does not involve an increase of joy. Pain results from a lack of adjustment, but not from a scarcity of functions. Hence if we strive for progress alone, we are moved not by the hope for greater joy, but by an enthusiastic belief in the value of progress and development itself. Does a socialistic order secure a more forceful, a more spontaneous, a more many-sided, or even a more harmonious growing of new demands and of new means for fulfilment than the capitalistic system which holds us all to-day?

The psychologist certainly has no right to ask to be heard first, when this strictly economic aspect of the great social problem is emphasized. Industrial specialists, administrators of labour, politicians, and financiers stand nearest to the issue. But whatever they testify, they ultimately have to point to mental facts, and the psychologist is naturally anxious to emphasize them. He has nothing new to contribute. [82] It is the old story of the stimulating influence of the spirit of competition. Healthy progress demands unusual exertion. All psychological conditions for that maximum strain are unfavourable in a socialistic state with its acknowledged need of rigid regulation and bureaucracy. We see all around us the flabby routine work, stale and uninspiring, wherever sharp rivalry has no chance. It is the great opportunity for mediocrity, while the unusual talent is made ineffective and wasted. Our present civilization shows that in every country really decisive achievement is found only in those fields which draw the strongest minds, and that they are drawn only where the greatest premiums are tempting them. To-day even the monopolist stands in the midst of such competition, as he can never monopolize the money of the land. This spur which the leaders feel is an incessant stimulus for all those whom they control, and, as soon as that tension is released at the highest point, a perfunctory performance with all its well-known side features, the waste and the idleness, the lack of originality and the unwillingness to take risks, must set in and deaden the work.

Nature runs gigantic risks all the time, and throws millions of blossoms away so as to have its harvest of fruit, and at the same time nature shows the strictest [83] economy and most perfect adjustment to ends in the single blossom which comes to fruit. Just this doubleness is needed in the progressive economic life. The rampant luxuriousness which is willing to throw away large means for a trial and for a fancy which may lead to nothing, and yet a scrupulous economy which reaches its ends with the smallest possible waste, must blend. But as long as man's mind is not greatly changed, both will be the natural tendency of the capitalist, and both are abhorred by the governmental worker. He has no right to run risks, but does not feel it his duty to avoid an unproductive luxuriousness. He wastes in the routine where he ought to economize, and is pedantic in the great schemes in which his imagination ought to be unbridled. The opponents of socialism have often likened the future state to a gigantic prison, where every one will be forced to do the work without a chance for a motive which appeals to him as an individual. This is in one respect unfair, as the socialists want to abolish private capital, but do not want to equalize the premiums for work. Yet is their method not introducing inequality up to the point where it has many of the bad features of our present system, and abolishing it just at the point where it would be stimulating and fertilizing to commerce and industry? We are to allow great [84] differences of personal possession. Even to-day the large companies count with hundred-thousand-dollar salaries, and there is nothing in the socialistic principle which would counteract this tendency. The differences may even grow, if the economic callings are to attract the great talents at all in such a future state. But just the one decisive value of the possessions for the development of industry and commerce—namely, the transforming of the material gain into the capital which produces and works, would become impossible. The national achievement would be dragged down. All the dangers which threaten bureaucratic industrialism everywhere—political party influences with their capricious zigzag courses, favouritism, protection and graft, waste and indifference, small men with inflated importance in great positions, and great men with crushed wings in narrow places—all would naturally increase, and weaken the nation in the rivalry of the world.

While such paralyzing influences were working from above, the changes from below would interfere no less with vigorous achievement. Every gateway would be wide open. Socialism would mean a policy opposite to that of the trade unions to-day. They are energetically excluding the unfit. Under the new order the fine [85] day for the unfit would have dawned. At present the socialists feel at home in the system of the unions, because the firm organization of the workingmen through the unions is helpful for their cause. But if that cause wins, the barriers of every union must break down, and the industrial energies of the nation will be scattered in the unimportant work in order to give an equal chance to the unproductive.

Nobody doubts that socialism would overcome some of the obvious weaknesses of the capitalistic era, and those weaknesses may be acknowledged even if we are faithful to our plan and abstract from mere human happiness. If only the objective achievement is our aim, we cannot deny that the million-fold misery from sickness and old age, from accidents at work, and from unemployment through a crisis in trade, from starvation wages, and from losses through fraudulent undertakings, is keeping us from the goal. But has the groaning of this misery remained unheard in these times, when capitalism has been reaching its height? The last two decades have shown that the system of private ownership can be in deepest harmony with all those efforts to alleviate its cruelties in order to strengthen the efficiency of the nation at work. Certainly the socialists themselves deserve credit for much in the [86] great international movement toward the material security of the workingman's social life. It is doubtful whether without her social democrats, Germany, the pioneer in the social insurance movement, would have given to the army of workingmen those protective laws which became the model for England and other nations, and which are beginning to be influential in American thinking, too. The laws against child labour, the efforts for minimum wage rates, and, most important, the worldwide tendency to secure a firm supervision and regulation of the private companies by the state, are characteristic features of the new period in which capitalism triumphs, and yet is freeing itself from cancerous growths which destroy its power for fullest achievement.

To work nine hours instead of ten, and eight instead of nine, was only apparently an encroachment on the industrial work. The worldwide experiment has proved that the shorter working hours allow an intensity of strain and an improvement of the workmen which ultimately heighten the value of the output. The safety devices burdened the manufacturer with expenses, and yet the economist knows that no outlay is more serviceable for the achievement of the factory. Unionism and arbitration treaties are sincere and momentous [87] efforts to help the whole industrial nation. And all this may be only the beginning. The time may really come when every healthy man will serve his year in the industrial army. Man and woman and child may thus be more and more protected against the destructive abuses of our economic scheme. Their physical health and their mental energy may be kept in better and better working order by social reforms, by state measures and strong organization. The fear of the future, that greatest destroyer of the labourer's working mood, may be more and more eliminated. Extremely much still remains to be done, but the best of it can surely be done without giving up the idea of private capital. In the framework of the capitalistic order such reforms mean a national scientific management in the interest of efficiency and success. If that framework is destroyed, the vigour and the energy are lost, and no improvements in the detail can patch up the ruinous weakness in the foundation. If the goal is an increased achievement of the industrialized nation, socialism is bound to be a failure as long as human minds and their motives are what they are to-day and what they have been through the last five thousand years.

No doubt such arguments have little weight with the larger number of those who come to the defence of [88] socialism. The purpose, they would say, is not at all to squeeze more work out of the nerves and muscles of the labourer, to fill still more the pocket of the corporations, to produce still more of the infernal noise in the workshops of the world. The real aim has nothing to do with the output and the muscle, but with the joy and happiness of the industrial workers, who have become slaves in the capitalistic era. It is quite true that if this is the end, the arguments which speak against the efficiency of socialism might well be disregarded. The mixing of the reasons can bring only confusion, and such chaos is unavoidable indeed, as long as the aims are not clearly discriminated. We may acknowledge frankly that the socialistic order may be a hindrance to highest efficiency, and yet should be welcomed because it would abolish the sources of unhappiness. Yet is there really any hope for such a paradise? The problem of achievement may stand nearer to the economist, but that of happiness and misery is thoroughly a question of the mind, and it is the duty of the psychologist to take a stand.

His issues, however, ought not to be confused by mixing in a side problem which is always emphasized when the emotional appeal is made and the misery of the workmen's fate is shown up. There is no unhappier [89] lot than that of those healthy men who can work and want to work, and do not find a chance to work. But this tremendous problem of the unemployed is not organically connected with the struggle about socialism. As far as social organization and human foresight can ever be able to overcome this disease of the industrial body, the remedies can just as well be applied in the midst of full-fledged capitalism. It is quite true that the misfortune of unemployment may never be completely uprooted, but vast improvements can easily be conceived without any economic revolution; and, above all, no scheme has been proposed by the socialists which would offer more. As long as there is a market with its ups and downs, as long as harvests vary and social depressions occur, there will be those who have no chance for their usual useful activity. If the community of the socialistic state supports them, it will do no more than the capitalistic state will surely do very soon, too. If we want to see clean issues, we ought to rule out the problem of unemployment entirely.

The socialistic hope can be only that, through the abolition of capital, the average workman will get a richer share from the fruits of his industrial labour. In the programmes of the American socialists it has taken the neat round figure that every workingman ought to [90] live on the standard of five thousand dollars yearly income. Of course the five thousand dollars themselves are not an end, but only a means to it. The end is happiness, and here alone begins the psychologist's interest. He does not discuss whether the five-thousand-dollar standard as minimum wage can really be expected. He asks himself only whether the goal can be reached, whether such a socialistic society would really secure a larger amount of human happiness. It is here that he answers that this claim is a psychological illusion. If we seek socialism for its external achievement we must recognize that it is a failure; if we seek it for its internal result, joy and happiness, it must be worse than a failure. The psychology of feeling is still the least developed part of our modern science of consciousness, but certain chief facts are acknowledged on all sides, and in their centre stands the law of the relativity of feeling. Satisfaction and dissatisfaction, content and discontent, happiness and unhappiness, do not depend upon absolute, but upon relative, conditions. We have no reason whatever to fancy that mankind served by the wonderful technique twenty centuries after Christ is happier than men were under the primitive conditions of twenty centuries before Christ. The level has changed and has steadily been raised, but [91] the feelings are dependent, not upon the height of the level, but upon the deviations from it. Each level brings its own demands in the human heart; and if they are fulfilled, there is happiness; and if they are not fulfilled, there is discontent. But the demands of which we know nothing do not make us miserable if they remain unfulfilled. It is the change, and not the possession, which has the emotional value. The up and down, the forward and backward, are felt in the social world, just as in the world of space the steady movement is not felt, but only the retardation or the acceleration.

The psychologist knows the interesting psychophysical law according to which the differences in the strength of our impressions are perceived as equal, not when the differences of the stimuli are really equal, but when the stimuli stand in the same relation. If we hear three voices, the sound has a certain intensity; if a fourth voice is added, the strength of the sound is swelling; we notice a difference. But if there is a chorus of thirty voices and one voice is added, we do not hear a difference at all. Even if five voices are added we do not notice it. Ten new singers must be brought in for us to hear the sound as really stronger. And if we have a mighty chorus of three hundred [92] singers, not even twenty or fifty or even eighty voices would help us to feel a difference; we need a hundred additional ones. In other words, the hundred singers which come to help the three hundred do not make more impression on us than the ten which are added to the thirty, or the one added to the three. Exactly this holds true for all our perceptions, for light and taste and touch. The differences upon which our pleasures and displeasures hang, obey this same law of consciousness. If we have three pennies, one added gives us a pleasure, one taken away gives us a displeasure, which is entirely different from the pleasure or displeasure if one penny is added or taken away from thirty or from three hundred pennies. In the possession of thirty, it needs a loss or gain of ten, in the possession of three hundred the addition or subtraction of a hundred, to bring us the same emotional excitement. A hundred dollars added to an income of five hundred gives us just as much joy as ten thousand added to fifty thousand dollars. The objective gain or loss does not mean anything; the relative increase or decrease decides human happiness.

Do we not see it everywhere in our surroundings? If we lean over the railing and watch the steerage in the crowded ship, is there really less gayety among the [93] fourth-class passengers than among the first-class? Where are the gifts of life which bring happiness to every one? I have friends to whom a cigar, a cocktail, and a game of cards are delightful sources of pleasure, the missing of which would mean to them a real deprivation. I have never played cards, I have never touched a cocktail, and have never had a cigar between my lips; and yet I have never missed them. On the other hand, I feel extremely uncomfortable if a day passes in which I have not gone through three or four newspapers, while I have friends who are most happy if they do not have a printed sheet in hand for months. The socialists claim that the possession of one's own house ought to be the minimum external standard, and yet the number increases of those who are not happy until they are rid of their own house and can live in a little apartment. Of course it might be said that the individual desires vary from man to man, but that an ample income allows every one to satisfy his particular likes and to protect himself against his particular dislikes. But the situation is not changed if we see it under this more general aspect of the money as means for the satisfaction of all possible wishes. The psychological law of the relativity of consciousness negates no less this general claim. There is no limit to the quantity of desires. On the [94] level of expensive life the desires become excessive, and only excessive means can satisfy them; on a lower economic level, the desires are modest, but modest means are therefore able to give complete satisfaction and happiness.

The greatest dissatisfaction, hopeless despair, expresses itself in suicide. Statistics show that those who sink to this lowest degree of life satisfaction are not the poorest. Not seldom they are the millionaires who have lost their fortune and kept only enough for a living which would still be a source of happiness to hosts of others. If the average wage were five thousand dollars, or, better said, the comfort which five thousand dollars can buy to-day, this standard would be taken as a matter of course like fresh air and fresh water. The same old dissatisfactions and discomforts would spring from the human heart, when it looked with envy on the luxuries of the ten-thousand-dollar men, or when by recklessness and foolishness or illness the habitual home life became suddenly reduced to a pitiable three-thousand-dollar standard, which would be the goal for the workingmen of to-day. We are too little aware that the average existence of the masses in earlier centuries was on a much narrower scale than the life of practically the poorest to-day, and that the mere material [95] existence of those who to-day consider themselves as industrial slaves is in many respects high above that of the apprentices in the periods before the machine age. Even at present those who think that they are at the bottom of material life in one country often live much better than the multitudes in other lands in which fewer desires have been aroused and developed.

The individual may often alternate between different standards, just as any one of us when he goes out camping may feel perfectly happy with the most moderate external conditions, which would appear to him utter deprivation in the midst of his stylish life the year around. Many an Irish servant girl feels that she cannot live here without her own bathroom, and yet is perfectly satisfied when she goes home for the summer and lives with seven in a room, not counting the pigs. This dependence upon relative conditions must be the more complete the more the income is used for external satisfactions. As far as the means serve education and æsthetic enjoyment and inner culture, there remains at least a certain parallelism between the amount of supply and the enjoyment. But the average American of the five-thousand-dollar class spends four thousand nine hundred dollars on goods of a different order. Altogether his expenses are the house and the table, the [96] clothes of the women, and his runabout. In all these lines there is no limit, and the house of to-day is no longer a pleasure if his neighbour builds a bigger one to-morrow. The man with the fifty-thousand-dollar expenditures feels the same dissatisfaction if he cannot have the steam yacht and the picture gallery which the multimillionaire enjoys.

The inner attitude, the temperament, the training, the adjustment of desires to the available means, is the only decisive factor in such situations. The trust magnate and the factory foreman have equal chances to feel happiness in the standard of life in which they live. If they compare themselves with those who are richer, and if their hearts hang on the external satisfactions, they both may feel wretched; and yet with another turn of mind they both may be content. Optimism and pessimism, contentment and envy, self-dependence and dependence upon the judgment of the world, joyfulness and despondency, are more decisive contrasts for the budget of happiness than the difference between fifteen dollars a week and fifteen dollars a minute. Some of my best friends have to live from hand to mouth, and some are multimillionaires. I have found them on the whole equally happy and equally satisfied with their position in life. If there was a difference at [97] all, I discovered that those who ate from silver plates were sometimes complaining about the materialism of our time, in which so much value is put on money. I have never found their fate especially enviable, nor that of the others especially pitiable, and evidently they themselves have no such feelings. The general impression is much more as if actors play on the stage. The one gives the rôle of the king in purple cloak and ermine, the other plays the part of a beggar in ragged clothes. But the one rôle is not more interesting than the other, and everything depends upon the art of playing the character.

This whole scramble for money's worth is based on a psychological illusion, not only because pleasure and displeasure are dependent upon relative conditions, but also because the elimination of one source of feeling intensifies the feelings from other sources. The vulgar display of wealth which cheapens our life so much, the desire to seek social distinction by a scale of expenditure which in itself gives no joy, have in our time accentuated the longing for wealth out of all proportion. This is true of every layer of society. The clerk's wife spends for her frocks just as absurdly large a part of his income as the banker's wife. Every salesgirl must have a plume on her hat rather than a nourishing luncheon. [98] Others must have six motor cars instead of a decent library in their palace. But this longing for useless display is still outdone by the hysterical craving for amusement. The factory girl must have her movies every night, and besides the nine hundred kino shows, a hundred and twenty theatres are needed to satisfy the amusement seeking crowd of New York, in addition to the half dozen which offer art. This mad race to outdo one another and this hunting after pleasures which tickle the senses have benumbed the social mind and have inhibited in it the feeling for deeper values. But if by a magic word extreme equality of material means were created and the mere sensuous enjoyments evenly distributed, in that moment all the other differences from individual to individual would be felt with heightened sharpness, and would be causes for much stronger feelings of happiness and unhappiness.

Men differ in their inborn mental powers, in their intelligence and talent, in beauty, in health, in honours and career, in family and friends. The contrasts which are created in every one of these respects are far greater and for the ill-fated far more cruel than those of the tax-payers. The beautiful face which is a passport through life and the discouraging homeliness, the perfect body which allows vigorous work and the weak organism of [99] the invalid unfit for the struggle of life, the genius in science or art or statesmanship and the hopelessly trivial mind, the youth in a harmonious, beautiful family life and the childhood in an atmosphere of discord, the home full of love from wife and children and the house childless and chilly, the honours of the community and the disappointment of social bankruptcy—they are the great premiums and the great punishments, which are whirled by fate into the crowd of mankind. Even here most of it is relative. We rejoice in four-score years, but if we knew that others were allowed a thousand years of life, we should be despondent that hardly a short century is dealt out to us. We are happy in the respect of our social community simply because we do not desire the honours of the czar or of the mikado. But if we began to measure our fate by that of others, how could we ever be satisfied? Women might envy men and men might envy women, the poet might wish to be the champion of sport and the sportsman might be unhappy because he is not a poet. No one of us can have the knowledge and the technical powers which the child of the thirtieth century will enjoy. As soon as we begin to compare and do not find the centre of our life in ourselves, we are condemned.

Everybody's life is composed of joys and pains which [100] may come from any of these sources. Where beauty is lacking, wit may brilliantly shine; where health is failing, a talent may console; where the family life is unhappy, the ambitions for a career may be fulfilled. Much inequality will thus result, but the chances for a certain evenness of human joy and sorrow will be the greater the more numerous the sources from which the joys and griefs of our days are springing. Add the inequalities of wealth, and you increase the chances that the emotional values in the lives of all of us will become more equal. The ugly girl may be rich and the poor one may be beautiful, the genius may hunger and the stupid man may marry the widow with millions, the healthy man may have to earn his scanty living and the patient may enjoy the luxuries of life. Their states of feeling will be more alike than if a socialistic order had put them all on the same economic level of philistine comfort. The joys of capital are after all much less deeply felt than any of those others, and the sufferings from poverty are much less incisive than those from disappointed ambition, from jealousy, from illness, or from bereavement. It is well known that many more people die from overfeeding than from underfeeding. We may feel disgusted that the luxuries so often fall to the unworthy and that the finest people [101] have to endure the hardship of narrow means. But all those other gifts and deprivations, those talents and beauties and powers and family relations, are no less arbitrarily dealt out. We all may wish to be geniuses or radiant beauties, great singers or fathers of a dozen children; we have not chosen our more modest lot.

It might be answered that the poverty of the industrial masses to-day means not only the absence of the special comforts, but that it means positive suffering. Men are starving from want and are chained down like slaves to a torturing task. But let us discriminate. It is true in states of unemployment and illness the physical man may be crushed by naked poverty, but that has nothing whatever to do with socialism. We have emphasized before that it is the solemn duty of society to find ways and means to protect every one who is willing to work as long as he is healthy, against starvation in times of old age and sickness, and if possible in periods of market depression. The non-socialistic community has the power to take care of that, and it is entirely an illusory belief that socialism has in that respect any advantage. All the comparisons of the two economic orders ought to refer only to the variations rather high above the starvation line, even though the American must call starvation a standard which the [102] coolie may think tolerable and to which the European poor in the Middle Ages were often accustomed. On the other hand, neither capitalism nor socialism can protect the reckless and the wasteful against economic suicide.

Much more important is the problem of suffering through the character of the work itself. That is the real fountainhead of the socialistic flood which threatens to inundate our present-day social structures. But is there not even here a psychological misunderstanding involved? It may be granted that many a man and many a woman stand in the factory day after day and year after year with the one feeling of distress and wretchedness at the hard work to which they are forced. But is their work really responsible for it, and is it not rather their personal attitude? Who is doing harder physical work than the sportsman? There is no more exhausting muscle strain than the climb over the glaciers of the Alps, which thousands pursue with passion. Analyze the profession of the physician. How many of his functions are in themselves of such a character that they might be denounced as the most humiliating slavery, if they were demanded from any man who could not see the aim and higher interest which they are serving! This is exactly the point [103] where the leaders of labour are sinning unpardonably. They work with all the means of suggestion, until the workman, as if hypnotized, looks on the mere movements which he is to perform in the factory, and forgets entirely the higher interest and aim of civilization which he is helping to serve. The scholar in his laboratory has to do a thousand things which in themselves are ugly and dirty, tiresome and dangerous, uninteresting and exhausting, but which he is performing with enthusiasm because he knows that he is serving the great ideal of cultured life, to discover the truth and thus to help the progress of mankind. There is under no factory roof a workman so forlorn that the work of his hands is not aiding the fulfilment of an equally great and equally ideal purpose of civilized mankind, the development of economic civilization. As soon as his labour amidst the noise of the machines is felt as such a service to an ideal cultural purpose, the work is no longer dead, but living, interesting, significant, wonderful.

The mother who takes care of her little children has to go through a thousand tiresome actions which would be intolerable if they were meaningless, but which compose a beautiful life if they are held together by the aim which the motherly love sees before it. Whatever work [104] a human being may perform, force on his mind the treacherous suggestion that it is meaningless, that it is slavery, that others seize the profit, and he must hate it and feel it an unbearable hardship. It has often been observed that the most bitter complaints have always come from those workers who are reached by the suggestions of theories and not from those who simply face practice, even though their life may be a much harder one. In Russia the workingmen of the city found their life so intolerable that revolts broke out, while the rural classes were satisfied with conditions of much more cruel deprivation. Our social reformers too easily forget the one great teaching of the history of mankind, that the most powerful factor in the world is the ideas. Surely there is some truth even in that one-sided picture of the history of civilization which makes everything dependent upon economic conditions, but the element of truth which is contained therein is due to the fact that economic conditions may influence the ideas. The ideas are the really decisive agencies. Only for ideas have men been ready to die, and for ideas have they killed one another. Give to the world the idea that earthly goods are useless and heavenly goods alone valuable, and in this kingdom of the religious idea the beggarly rags of the monk are more desired than the [105] gold of the mighty. Religion and patriotism, honour and loyalty, ambition and love, reform ideals and political goals, æsthetic, intellectual, and moral ideas have turned the great wheel of history. Give to the workingman the right kind of ideas, the right attitude toward his work, and all the hardship becomes blessedness and the suffering glory. His best payment then will be the satisfaction of carrying his stone to the great temple of human progress, even though it may not be a cornerstone.

Even the complaint repeated without end that the workingman's task is unendurable because of its unceasing monotony is ultimately nothing but a psychological theory, and this theory is superficial and misleading. It is easy to point out to the suggestible mind that there is a wonderful enrichment of life in variety, and that uniformity must therefore be something ugly and discouraging and unworthy. But the real mental facts allow just as well the opposite argument. The mere change and variation, going from one thing to another, makes the mind restless and distracted, without inner unity and harmony. To be loyal to one task and to continue it faithfully and insistently, brings that perfect adjustment of the mind in which every new act is welcome because it has become the habit ingrained in [106] the personality. To be sure there are individual differences. We have in political life, too, radicals who get more satisfaction from change, and conservatives who prefer continuity of traditions; and so the whole mental structure of some men is better adjusted to a frequent variation in work, and that of others better prepared for continuity. The one has a temperament which may lead him from one occupation to another, from one town to another, from one flat to another, from one set of companions to another. But there is the opposite type of minds. To them it is far more welcome to continue throughout life at the same work, in the same old home, in touch with the same dear friends. Many minds surely are better fitted for alternation in their activities, but many others, and they certainly are not the worst, are naturally much better adapted to a regular repetition. There are opportunities for both types of mental behaviour in the workshop of the nation, and the peaceful adjustment is disturbed only by the hasty theory that repetition is a lower class of work, which makes man a mere machine and that it is therefore to be despised. Change the theory about uniformity, and you remove monotony from the industrial world. Monotony is only the uniformity which is hated.

Do we not see that power of theories and ideas every [107] where around us, even in the most trivial things? The most splendid gown is nothing but an object of contempt if it is the fashion of the day before yesterday. In lands where titles and decorations are a traditional idea, the little piece of tin may be more coveted than any treasures of wealth. Through ideas only can the great social question be solved. No distribution of income can change in the least the total sum of pleasure and displeasure in the world, and the socialistic scheme is of all the useless efforts to increase pleasure and to decrease displeasure the least desirable, because it works, as we have seen, at the same time against those mental functions which secure the most forceful progress of economic life. A true change can come only from within. The superficial, unpsychological theories of human happiness, which have been hammered into the working population of our age, have made true happiness more and more difficult to attain. There is small chance that this inner conversion will come in our day through religion, however much religion may help toward it. There is still smaller chance that philosophy can do it and that the average man will take the attitude of Antisthenes who claimed that it is divine not to need anything and that he who needs least is nearest to the ideal. But there is every chance that mankind [108] will remember again more vividly the deeper lasting values of humanity. Society must be sobered after the frenzy of this present-day rush for external goods. The shallow disappointment is felt too widely already. The world is beginning to discover once more that this scramble for pearls and palaces and motor cars among the rich, and for their showy imitations among the middle class, and the envy of material profits and the chase for amusements even among the poorest, leave life meaningless and cold and silly. As soon as the industrial community turns to a new set of ideas and becomes inspired by the belief in the ideal value of the work as work and as a necessary contribution to the progress of mankind, the social question will be solved, as all the differences which socialism wants to eliminate then appear trivial and insignificant.

But on the other hand, this belief cannot grow, and cannot spread its roots deep in the soil of the industrial mind unless, as a necessary counterpart, the ideas of duties and obligations spread and enlarge among those who profit from the rights of capital. The capitalistic society must organize itself so that the sinking below the starvation line through illness, old age, or unemployment will be reduced to a minimum, so that the greatest possible participation in all which gives higher value to [109] life will be secured for the worker and his family, and above all, so that the industrial control will be exerted by the best and the wisest. Nowhere is reform of ideals more needed. The brutality of capital is never felt more strongly than when the workingman suspects that those at the top are not selected on account of their stronger capacities. Only when capital is conscious of its duties can the belief in the ideal meaning of the workingman's function take hold of the masses and inhibit the suggestion of socialism. Merely granting the external claims, giving to the factory girls increasing chance for amusement, means to deceive them. The more such longings are satisfied, the more they must grow and become a craze which sharpens the feeling of dissatisfaction. This desire for superficial joys, for sensual amusements and cheap display is nothing but a suggested habit, which imitation creates in a period of waste. If a time of simplicity were to come, not only the longing for these prizes would become silent, but the prizes themselves would appear worthless. Liberate the workingman from his distrust of the present social order; let him feel deeply that his duties are not enforced slavery but a solemn offering to human progress, which he gives in glad coöperation in the spirit of ideal belief. At the same time stop the overestimation [110] of the outer enjoyments, and cultivate the appreciation of the lasting values, and our time of unrest will come to inner harmony. But do not believe that this can ever be done, if those who are called to be the leaders of the social group are not models and do not by their own lives give the cue for this new attitude and new valuation. As long as they outdo one another in the wild chase of frivolity and seek in the industrial work of the nation only a stronghold for their rights and not a fountain spring of duties, as long as they want to [111] enjoy instead of to believe, this inner change can never come in the community. The psychologist can do nothing but to predict that no other scheme, no outer reform, no new plan of distribution, can bring a real change, as every calculation which works with outer means to secure happiness must remain a psychological illusion. The change from within is the only promise and the only hope. [112]

III [113]

THE INTELLECTUAL UNDERWORLD

The public conscience of the social world has been stirred in recent days by the dangers which threaten from an antisocial world that lurks in darkness. The sociologists recognize that it is not a question of vicious and criminal individuals, but one of an antisocial atmosphere, of immoral traditions and surroundings, through which crime flourishes and vice is fostered. They speak of a social underworld, and mean by it that whole pitiable setting in which the gangs of thieves and the hordes of prostitutes live their miserable lives. The public discussions nowadays are full of stirring outcries against the rapid spreading of vice in our large cities; it is a war for clean living and health. But after all we ought not to forget that similar dangers surround our inner culture and our spiritual life, and that an intellectual underworld threatens our time, which demands a no less rigorous fight until its vice is wiped out. The vice of the social underworld gives a sham satisfaction [114] to the human desire for sensual life; the vice of the intellectual underworld gives the same sham fulfilment to the human longing for knowledge and for truth. The infectious germs which it spreads in the realm of culture may ultimately be more dangerous to the inner health of the nation than any physical diseases. The battle against vice and crime in the world of the body ought to be paralleled by a battle against superstition and humbug in the world of the mind. The victory over the social underworld would anyhow never be lasting unless the intellectual under-world were subjugated first. In the atmosphere of sham-truth all the antisocial instincts grow rankly.

I know of a large, beautiful high school in which the boys and girls are to receive the decisive impulses for their inner life from well-trained teachers who have had a solid college education. I have found out that quite a number of these teachers are clients of a medium who habitually informs them as to their future, and for a dollar a sitting gives them advice at every turn of their lives. I do not know whether she takes it from the tea leaves or from an Egyptian dream book or from her own trance fancies, but I do know that the prophecies of this fraud have deeply influenced some of their lives and shaped the faculty of the high school. What does [115] this mean? Mature educators to whose training society has devoted its fullest effort and who are chosen to bring to the youth the message of earnest thought and solid knowledge, and whose intellectual life ought therefore to be controlled by consistent thinking and real love for knowledge, fall back into the lowest forms of mental barbarism and really believe in the most illogical prostitution of truth. The double life of Jekyll and Hyde is more natural than this. The impulse to virtuous behaviour and the atrocities of the criminal may after all be combined in one character, but the desire to master the world by a disciplined knowledge and to think the universe in ideas of order and law cannot go together with a real satisfaction and belief in the chaotic superstitions of mediumistic humbugs. Here we have truly a twofold personality, one living in a world of culture and the other in an underworld of intellectual dissipation and vice. It would not be desirable for the high school teachers who are to be models of virtue to live a second life as gamblers and pick-pockets, but it is more dangerous if they are the agents of intellectual culture and indulge at the same time in intellectual prostitution.

No spirit of false tolerance ought any longer to be permitted, when the treacherous danger has become so [116] nation wide. It is sufficient to take up any newspaper between New York and San Francisco and run through the advertisements of the spiritualists and psychical mediums, the palmists and the astrologers, the spiritual advisers and the psychotherapists: it is evident that it is a regular organized industry which brings its steady income to thousands, and which in the bigger towns has its red-light districts with its resorts for the intellectual vice. The servant girl gets her information as to the fidelity of her lover for fifty cents, the clerk who wants to bet on the races pays five dollars, the great banker who wants to bet on stocks pays fifty dollars for his prophetic tips, and the widow who wants messages from her husband pays five hundred dollars, but they all come and pay gladly. If this mood permeates the public of all classes, it is not surprising that the cheapest spiritualistic fraud creeps into religious circles, that the wildest medical humbug is successfully rivalling the work of the scientific physician, and that the intellectual graft of psychical research is beginning to corrupt the camps of the educated. Surely it is a profitable business, and I know it from inside information, as not long ago a very successful clairvoyant came to the Harvard Psychological Laboratory and offered me a partnership with half his income, not because he himself believed [117] much in my psychology, but because, as he assured me, there are some clients who think more highly of my style of psychology than of his, and if we got together the business would flourish. He told me just how it was to be done and how easy it is and what persons frequent his parlours. But I have inside information of a very different kind before me, if I think of the victims who come to me for help when superstition has broken their mental springs. There was a young girl to whom life was one great joy, until for ten dollars she got the information that she would die in a very big building, and now she goes into hysterics when her family tries to take her into a theatre or a hotel or a railway station or a school.

Indeed the psychologist has an unusually good chance to get glimpses of this filthy underworld, even if he does not frequent the squalid quarters of the astrologers. Bushels of mail bring this superstition and mental crookedness to his study, and his material allows him to observe every variety of illogical thought. If a letter comes to his collection which presents itself as a new specimen that ought to be analyzed a little further, nothing is needed but a short word of reply. It will at once bring a full supply of twisted thought, sufficient for a careful dissection. It has been said repeatedly [118] in the various vice investigations that no one can understand the ill fate of the vicious girls, unless he studies carefully the men whom they are to please. An investigation into mental vice demands still more an understanding of those minds which play the part of customers. There are too many who cannot think in straight lines and to whom the most absurd linking of facts is the most satisfactory answer in any question. The crudeness of their intellect, which may go together with ample knowledge in other fields, predestines them to be deceived and puts a premium on the imposture. I may try to characterize some varieties of crooked thinking from chance tests of the correspondence with which the underworld has besieged me. I have only the letters of most recent date in hand.

I abstract, of course, from those written by insane individuals. They come plentifully and show all sorts of distortions and impossible ideas. But they do not belong here. The confused mind of the patient is not to be held responsible. His absurdities are symptoms of disease, and they are sharply to be separated from the lack of logic in the sound mind, just as the impulse to kill in paranoia is to be distinguished from the murderous schemes of the criminal. It is generally not difficult to recognize at once which is which. I find the most frequent [119] type of letters from evidently diseased persons to be writings like this: "Dear Sir: I wish to let you know that some young men have a sort of a comb machine composed of wireless telephone and reinforced electricity. They can play this machine and make a person talk or wake or go to sleep. They can tell where you are, even miles away. They play in the eyes and brain, I think. They have two machines; so they know when the police or anybody is coming toward their house. They keep talking most of the time so as to take up a person's mind. It is about time it was stopped, but people don't understand such things around here. Could a wireless telephone get their voices? Hoping you will do something to stop them, I am yours, One Who Has Been Annoyed Very Much ."

There is no help for such a poor sufferer except in the asylum. Here we want to deal not with the patients, but only with the sinners who sin against logic, while their minds are undiseased.

There is another large class of correspondents, which is not to be blamed, and which is one of the most interesting contributors to the psychologist's files. People write long discussions of theories which they build up on peculiar happenings in their minds. The theories [120] themselves may be entirely illogical, or at least in contradiction to all acknowledged science, but such letters are interesting, because they disclose abnormal mental states. Here it is not real insanity; but all kinds of abnormal impulses or ideas, of psychasthenic emotions, of neurasthenic disturbances, of hysteric inhibition, are the starting points, and it is only natural that such pathological intrusions should bewilder the patient and induce him to form the wildest theories. Again, he may believe in the most improbable and most fantastic connection of things, but this is due to the overwhelming power of disturbances which he is indeed unable to explain to himself. I have a whole set of letters from women who explain in fantastic theories their magical power to foresee coming events; and yet it is not difficult to recognize as the foundation of all such ideas some well-known forms of memory disturbance. Commonly it is the widespread tendency of women to accompany a scene with the feeling that they have experienced it once before. They are few who never have had it, especially in states of fatigue; many have it very often; and some are led to trust it and to become convinced that they really experienced the scene, at least in their minds, beforehand. This uncanny impression then easily develops into untenable speculations on the [121] borderland of normal intellect. The letters which approach those of the insane most nearly come from persons who try to work out a theory to account for hysterical experiences which break into their normal life. Sometimes the most absurd explanations must be acknowledged as justified from the standpoint of the patient. A woman wrote to me that she had the abnormal power to produce railroad wrecks by her mere will, while she was lying at home in bed. She wanted me to hypnotize her in order to relieve her from this uncanny power. She had elaborated this thought in full detail. She did not know, what I found out only slowly, that in hysterical attacks at night, for which every memory was lost the next morning, she used a stolen switch key to open a switch, because she was angry with a railway official. I will ignore all such cases with an abnormal background here and confine myself to the healthy crowd.

If I were to characterize their writings from an outside point of view, I might first say that their expressions are expansive. There is no limit to their manuscripts, though I have to confess that an exposition of eighty-five hundred pages which has just been announced to me by its author has not yet reached me. Nor can it be denied that their relation to old-fashioned [122] or to new-fashioned spelling is not always a harmonious one. Nor should I call them always polite: the criticism of my own opinions, which they generally know only from some garbled newspaper reports, often takes forms which are not the usual ones for scholarly correspondence. "Whether it is your darkness or if it is the badness of the police that go around calling themselves the government, that probably ordered you to put such ignorance in the Sunday article, I do not know." Or more straightforward are letters of this type: "Greeting—You take the prize as an educated fool. According to reports to me by less stupid and more honest men than you, the matter is." It is surprising how often the handwriting is pretty, coquettish, or affected, but almost half of my crank correspondence is typewritten.

When the newspapers tell of a mysterious case, minds of this type immediately feel attracted to mix in. When a few years ago I published an article disclosing the tricks of Madame Palladino, I was simply flooded with letters of advice and of explanation. The same thing occurred recently when the papers reported that I was experimenting with Beulah Miller. Now it is easy to understand that those who fancied that the Miller child had supernatural gifts of telepathy and [123] clairvoyance would wish to bring their questions to me so that I might make Beulah Miller trace their lost bracelets or predict their fortune in the Stock Exchange. But I was at a loss to understand why so many persons from Maine to California felt tempted to write long letters to me in which they told me what kind of questions I ought to ask the child, as if I could not formulate a question for myself. Every one expected a special report for himself with exact statements of her answers. The whole performance showed a lack of judgment which is typical of that lower intellectual layer; and yet the letters were often written on beautifully monogrammed letter paper. More often, however, my own writings or doings have nothing to do with the case. I am the perfectly innocent receiver of written messages about anything between heaven and earth, while the messages which my correspondents receive from me are not always authentic. One of my psychically talented writers reports: "On May 31st at eight forty-nine A. M. in the midst of a thunderstorm I came into communication with Doctor Münsterberg and asked him to send me a message. He said, 'The name of my son is Wilhelm Münsterberg.'" It is improbable that I lied so boldly about my family, even in a telepathic message. [124]

I may select a few typical theories, which all come from evidently otherwise normal and harmless people. I have before me a whole series of manuscripts from a druggist who is sure that his ego theory is "very near the truth." It is in itself very simple and convincing. "The right and the left cerebral egos united with one sublime ego are in the body in a loose union in possession of an amœboid cell. During sleep they may separate. The sublime ego wanders through nerve paths to the bowels, and the bowel experiences are the dreams." An experiment brought a definite proof of this. The druggist dyed some crackers deep blue with methylene blue, and later dreamed that a large train of blue food was passing by. As each carriage of the train corresponded to a granule of starch in the crackers, he was able to figure that the ego which saw those parts of the crackers was about one thousandth of an inch large. "The fact of seeing in dreams is due to vital force, the peculiar low speed to the high vibration force of living albuminoids emitted from every tendril of bioplasm and perceived by the eye of the ego-bion during its visit." "Within the ego-bion is the ego itself, which is much simpler looking, about one hundredth of a micromillimeter." I do not want to go into details of how these egos can be transmitted "by kiss or otherwise [125] " from one generation to another, but I can say that as soon as the reader has grasped the fundamental thesis of the author, everything follows with perfect logic. The good man, who is doubtless a faithful druggist and whose mind is perfectly clear, has simply twisted some of the ideas which he has gathered from his ample reading and developed his pet theory.

His case is very similar to that of a dignified, elderly trained nurse who is faithfully devoted to her noble daily work and who follows her vocation without indicating to any one that she is the author of a great unpublished philosophical work. She has spent twenty-five years of her life on the elaboration of this *magnum opus*, which is richly illustrated. Everything in the book is consistent and in harmony with its presuppositions. The theory again is very simple; every detail is perfectly convincing, if you acknowledge the starting point. As to this, there may be difference of opinion. The fundamental thought is that all human souls are born in the forests of Central Africa. "Souls are sexless forces. Never is one soul born into life. There are always two. Often we find three pairs of almost the same type with but a shadow of density to distinguish each pair. Man evolutes upward on the scale of life by two tribes of apes. Ere man becomes human, he [126] represents one cell force. When man takes the human form as Maquake, he becomes a double life cell." I do not claim to be an expert in this system, but if I understand the whole work rightly, the idea is that any human soul born there by the monkeys in Africa has to pass in circles of one thousand years from individual to individual, becoming at first negro, then Indian, then Malayan, then Hindu, then Greek, Celt, and Roman, then Jew, and finally American. After a thousand years the soul begins to degenerate and enters sinners and criminals. Which stage the soul has reached can easily be seen from the finger nails. The chief illustrations of the great work were therefore drawings of finger nails of all races. It is a side issue of the theory that "souls once matured generally pass on to another star. The nearer the sun is to the star holding life, the denser is all growth in nature." I acknowledge that this view of evolution does not harmonize exactly with my own, but I cannot deny that the whole system is worked out with perfect consistency, and wherever I asked the writer difficult questions as to some special problems, she was at once ready to give the answers with completely logical deduction from her premises. She is by no means mentally diseased, and she does not mix her theories with her practical activity. If she sits [127] as nurse at the bedside of a patient, she recognizes of course from the finger nails that this particular soul may be three or five thousand years old, and accordingly in a decaying state, but that does not interfere with her conscientious work as a nurse and helper.

To be sure, not every one spends twenty-five years on the elaboration of some twisted fancies. Most of my correspondents write the monumental thoughts of their systems with decisive brevity. A physician informs me that every thought and act of our lives is transfixed on the etheric vapours that surround our earth, and that it is therefore only natural that a clairvoyant is able to see those fixed events and write them down afterward from the ethereal inscriptions. Another tells about his discovery that the human body is a great electrical magnet. I am the more glad to make this fact widely known, as the author writes that he has not given it to the public yet, as he is not financially able to advertise it. Yet he himself adds that after all it is not necessary to advertise truth. On eight quarto pages he draws the most evident consequences of his discovery and shows how he is able to explain by it the chemical change of each cell in the brain and to prove that "foolish so-called spirits are simply electrical demonstrations." "I can demonstrate [128] every current, nerve cell, and atom of the human body. It may seem strange to you that I claim so much, but with the induction every investigation has been so easy for me. I have never been puzzled for any demonstration yet, but I am still searching for more knowledge. Yours for investigation." I may say that this is a feature common to most of my correspondents of this metaphysical type. They are never "puzzled."

Nearly related to this type of theories are the systems of astrology; and in our upper world very few are really aware what a rôle astrology is still playing in the intellectual underworld. Some of the astrological communications I receive periodically go so far beyond my understanding that I do not even dare to quote them. But some of the astrological authors present very neat and clean theories which are so simple and so practical that it is almost a pity that they are absurd. For instance, I am greatly interested in the question of determining how far the mind of individuals is predisposed for particular vocations, and in the psychological laboratory we are busy with methods to approach the problem. The astrologers have a much more convincing scheme. My friend writes that he has observed "over two thousand cases wherein the dates of [129] birth have been the means to give the position of the planets at the hour of birth, the purpose being to ascertain the influence they had on man. Now the furniture business calls for an artistic temperament, and after careful observation through birth dates it is found that the successful furniture men have the planet Venus in their nativities. But the Venus influence is prominent also in other lines of business such as art, jewellery, and in all lines where women's necessities are manufactured. Other planetary influences on success in business are: Saturn for miners, tanners, gardeners, clowns, and beggars; Mercury for teachers, secretaries, stationers, printers, and tailors; Jupiter for clergymen, judges, lawyers, and senators; Mars for dentists, barbers, cutlers, carpenters, and apothecaries; Uranus for inventors, chemists, occultists, and others."

One system which is still more frequent than the astrological is the strictly spiritualistic one, which expresses itself in spirit returns and messages from the other world. Geographically the most favoured stations for wireless heavenly connections seem to be Brooklyn, New York, and Los Angeles, California. The adherents of this underworld philosophy have a slang of their own, and the result is that their letters, while they spring from the deepest emotions, sound as [130] if they were copied from the same sample book. The better style begins about like this: "Knowing that you are intensely interested in things psychological, I beg to enclose you copies of some of the automatic letters which I have received. I have a young lawyer friend in the city, and he and I can throw down fifteen or twenty sheets of paper on a table, take hold of hands and get them written full, and in this way I have received letters from Pericles, Aristides, Immanuel Kant, and many others. I got letters from Julia Ward Howe a week after her transition, and I got letters from Emerson and Abraham Lincoln by asking for them. I enclose copy of the last letter which I received from Charlotte Cushman, and I think you will agree there is nothing foolish about it or indeed about any of the letters. I have recently married again, and my present wife is a wonderful trance medium, probably the best means of communication between the two worlds living to-day." This is not exceptional, as practically every one of my spiritualistic correspondents has some "best means of communication between the two worlds." The messages themselves usually begin: "My loved one, out of the realms of light and truth, I come to you ." and so on. If the letters do not come from the spiritualists themselves, some of their friends feel the need of [131] turning my attention to the "wonderful psychic powers" of their acquaintances. Not seldom the spirits take a more refined form. "The forms of the newly dead come to me in bulk. I see and feel them. They are purplish inky in colour. When a real spirit comes to me in white, I close my eyes. I seem to have to. The spirit or presence most commonly seen, I believe, is a thought form. It frequently comes off the cover of a magazine, and were I not getting wise, I would think the universe turned suddenly to beauty. But I am learning that a person can receive wonderfully exaggerated reports from the very soul of the artist."

From here we see before us the wide vista of the individual gifts and talents: the underworld people are sometimes bragging of them, sometimes grafting with them, if not blackmailing, and often simply enjoying them with the sweet feeling of superiority. The powers turn in all valuable directions. Here is one who wishes to know whether I have ever heard of any other "person who senses the magnetism of the earth and is able to tell many kinds of earthquakes? Also volcanic heats? A quick reply will favour me." Many have the regular prophetic gift; practically every one of them foresaw the assassination of McKinley. Most of them, however, are gifted in curing diseases. The typical [132] letter reads as follows: "There is a young man living here who seems to be endowed with a wonderful occult power by the use of which he is able to diagnose almost any human ailment. He goes into a trance, and while in this condition the name of the subject is given him, and then without any further questions he proceeds to diagnose his case fully and correctly and prescribes a treatment for the relief of the trouble. In every case yet diagnosed a cure has almost immediately resulted." This kind of gift is so frequent that it is really surprising that so many physicians still rely on their clumsier method. Marvellous also are the effects which hypnotism can secure in this paradise of the ignorant. After having hypnotized patients many hundred times, I fancied that I had a general impression as to the powers and limits of hypnotism. But there is no end to the new information which I get from my hypnotizing correspondents. "Has it ever occurred to you that by hypnotism death will be prevented, and all ills, mental or otherwise, be cured before long? Why do I think so?" Of course I do not know why she thinks so. I usually do not know why the writers of the underworld letters think so. Or rather I usually do know that they do not think at all.

There may be many who will read all this not only [133] with surprise, but with skepticism. They live their intellectually clean lives, dwell in safe, comfortable houses of the intellect and move on well-paved educational streets, and never see or hear anything of those inhabitants of the intellectual slums. If ever a letter like those which pour in hundreds to the desk of the psychologist were to stray into their mail, they would feel sure that they had to do with a lunatic who belongs in an asylum under a physician's care. They have no idea that not only their furnaceman and washwoman, but also their tailor and their watchmaker, or perhaps the teacher of their children, and, if they examine more carefully, three of their last dinner guests, are strolling for hours or for a night, or living for seasons, if not for a lifetime, in that world of superstition and anti-intellectual mentality. Such people are not ill; they are personally not even cranks; they are simply confused and unable to live an ordered intellectual life. Their character and temperament and their personality in every other respect may be faultless, but their ideas are chaotic. They bring together the contradictory and make contrasts out of the identical, and, far from any sound religious belief or any true metaphysical philosophy, they simply mix any mystical whims into the groups of thought which civilization has brought into [134] systematic order. Instead of trying to learn, they are always longing for some illegitimate intellectual profit; they are always trying to pick the pocket of the absolute.

It is not difficult to recognize the social conditions from which this tendency springs. The fundamental one, after all, is the widely spread lack of respect for the expert. Such a lack easily results from democratic life, as democracy encourages the belief that every one can judge about everything and can decide from his own resources what ought to be thought and what ought to be done. Yet no one can claim that it is truly a part of democracy itself and that the democratic spirit would suffer if this view were suppressed. On the contrary, democracy can never be fully successful and can never be carried through in consistent purity until this greatest danger of the democratic spirit of society is completely overcome and repressed by an honest respect for the expert and a willing subordination of judgment to his better knowledge. Another condition which makes our country a favourite playground for fantastic vagaries is the strong emphasis on the material sides of life, on business and business success. The result is a kind of contrast effect. As the surface of such a rushing business life lacks everything which would satisfy the [135] deeper longings of the soul, the effort to create an inner world is readily pushed to mystical extremes in which all contact with the practical world is lost, and finally all solid knowledge disregarded and caricatured. The newspapers have their great share, too. Any absurdity which a crank anywhere in the world brings forth is heralded with a joy in the sensational impossibilities which must devastate the mind of the naïve reader.

But whatever the sources of this prevailing superstition may be, there ought to be no disagreement about its intellectual sinfulness and its danger to society. We see some alarming consequences in the growth of the revolt against scientific medicine. Millions of good Americans do not want to know anything about physicians who have devoted their lives to the study of medicine, but prefer any quack or humbug, any healer or mystic. Yet for a queer reason the case of the treatment of diseases shows the ruinous results of this social procedure very slowly. Every scientific physician knows that many diseases can be cured by autosuggestion in emotional excitement, and if this belief in the quack produces the excitement and the suggestion, the patient may really be cured, not on account but in spite of the quack who treats him. The whole misery of this antimedical movement is therefore somewhat veiled and [136] alleviated. But this is not so in the fields of real culture and knowledge. The belief in the absurdities there has not even an autosuggestive value. It is simply destructive to the life of civilized society. It is absurd for us to put our best energies to work to build up a splendid system of education for the youth of the whole nation, and at the same time to allow its structure to be undermined by the millionfold intellectual depravity.

Of course it may be difficult to say what ought to be done. I feel sure that society ought to suppress with relentless energy all those parlours of the astrologists and palmists, of the scientific mediums and spiritualists, of the quacks and prophets. Their announcements by signs or in the public press ought to be stopped, and ought to be treated by the postal department of the government as the advertisements of other fraudulent enterprises are treated. A large rôle in the campaign would have to be played by the newspapers, but their best help would be rendered by negative action, by not publishing anything of a superstitious and mystical type. The most important part of the fight, however, is to recognize the danger clearly, to acknowledge it frankly, and to see with open eyes how alarmingly the evil has grown around us. No one will fancy that any [137] social schemes can be sufficient to bring superstition to [138] an end, any more than any one can expect that the present fight against city vice will forever put a stop to sexual immorality. But that surely cannot be an argument [139] for giving up the battle against the moral perversities of metropolitan life. The fact that we cannot be entirely successful ought still less to be an argument for any leniency with the intellectual perversities and the infectious diseases the germs of which are disseminated [140] in our world of honest culture by the inhabitants of the cultural underworld.

IV [141]

THOUGHT TRANSFERENCE

The harmony and soundness of society depend upon its inner unity of mind. Social organization does not mean only an external fitting together, but an internal equality of mind. Men must understand one another in order to form a social unit, and such understanding certainly means more than using the same words and the same grammar. They must be able to grasp other men's point of view, they must have a common world in which to work, and this demands that they mould the world in the same forms of thought. If one calls green what another calls sour, and one feels as noise what another feels as toothache, they cannot enter into a social group. Yet it is no less confusing and no less antisocial if the world which one sees as a system of causes and effects is to another a realm of capricious, causeless, zigzag happenings. The mental links which join society are threatened if some live with their thoughts in a world of order and natural law, and others in a mystical chaos. [142]

This has nothing to do with differences of opinion. Society profits from contrasting views, from discussion and struggle. The opposing parties in a real debate understand each other well and are working with the same logic and the same desire for order of thought. This contrast between order and mysticism has still less to do with the difference of knowledge and belief in a higher religious and philosophical sense. There is no real antagonism between science and religion, between experience and philosophical speculation. They point to each other, they demand each other, and no social question is involved when the interests of one man emphasize more the scholarly search for scientific truth, and those of another concentrate throughout his lifework on the emotional wisdom of religion. It is quite different with mysticism and science; they are not two parties of a debate on equal terms. They exclude each other, as the mystic projects his feeling interests into those objects which the scientist tries to analyze and to understand as effects of causes. Nothing is a safer test of the cultural development of a society than the instinct for the difference between religion and superstition. Mysticism is a systematized superstition. It never undermines the true interests of society more than when it goes to work [143] with pseudo-scientific tools. Its most repellent form, that of sheer spiritualism, has in recent years declined somewhat, and the organizations for antilogical, psychical research eke out a pitiable existence nowadays. But the community of the silent or noisy believers in telepathy, mystical foresight, clairvoyance, and wonder workers seems to increase.

The scientific psychologist might have a twofold contact with such movements. His most natural interest is that of studying the mental makeup of those who chase this will-o'-the-wisp. Their mental vagaries and superstitious fancies are quite fascinating material for his dissection. But for the interests of society an entirely different effort is, after all, more consequential. The psychologist has no right to avoid the trouble of examining conspicuous cases which superficially seem to endorse the fantastic theories of the mentally untrained. Such an investigation is his share, as indeed mental occurrences generally stand in the centre of the alleged wonderful facts. From this feeling of social responsibility some years ago I approached the hysterical trickster, Madame Palladino, who had so much inflamed the mystical imagination of the country, and from this interest in the social aspect I undertook again recently a research into the mental powers of Beulah [144] Miller, who was well on the way to bewilder the whole nation and thus to stir up the always latent mystic inclinations of the community. It is a typical specimen of those cases which can easily upset the loosely reasoning public and do tremendous harm to the mental unity of the social organism. It seems worth while to illuminate it in full detail.

Indeed, since the days when Madame Eusapia Palladino stirred the whole country with her marvellous mystic powers, no case of psychical mystery has engaged the interest of the nation as that of little Beulah Miller in Warren, Rhode Island, has done. The story of her wonderful performances has become a favourite feature of the Sunday papers, and the small New England town for the first time in its long history has been in the limelight. The reporters have made their pilgrimages, and every one has returned bewildered and amazed. Here at last the truth of telepathy was proved. Sworn affidavits of reliable persons removed the last doubts; and I myself, with my long training as a scientist, had to confess, when for the first time I had spent a few hours with Beulah Miller, that I was as deeply startled and overcome with wonder as I was after the first night with Eusapia Palladino. Yet what a contrast! There the elderly, stout Italian woman at a [145] midnight hour, in dimly lighted rooms, in disreputable New York quarters, where the palmists and mediums live in their world of sham psychology, sitting in a trance state at a table surrounded by spiritualistic believers who had to pay their entrance fees; here a little, naïve, ten-year-old girl among her toys in the kitchen of her parents' modest white cottage in a lovely country village! I never felt a more uncanny, nerve-irritating atmosphere than in Palladino's squalid quarters, and I do not remember more idyllic, peaceful surroundings than when I sat between Beulah and her sister through bright sunny mornings in their mother's home with their cat beside them and the pet lamb coming into the room from the meadow. There everything suggested fraud, and when at my second séance her foot was caught behind the curtain and the whole humbug exposed, it was exactly what I had expected. But here everything breathed sincerity and naïveté and absence of fraud—yet my mere assurance cannot convince a skeptic; we must examine the case carefully.

The claims are very simple: Here is a school child of ten years who is able to read in the mind of any one present anything of which he is thinking. If you take a card from a pack and look at it, and still better if several people look at it, and best of all if her mother [146] or sister looks at it, too, Beulah will say at once which card it is, although she may stand in the farthest corner of the room. She will give you the date on any coin which you have in hand; in a book she will tell you the particular word at which you are looking. Indeed, a sworn affidavit reports still more surprising feats. Beulah gave correctly the name of the reporter whom nobody else knew and the name of the New York paper for which she is writing. At school she reads words written on the blackboard with her back turned to it. At home she knows what any visitor is hiding in his pocket.

The serious-minded man who is disgusted with spiritualistic charlatans and their commercial humbug is naturally inclined here, too, at once to offer the theory that all is fraud and that a detective would be the right man to investigate the case. When the newspapers discovered that I had begun to study the girl, I received from many sides letters with suggestions to look for certain devices with which stage performers carry out such tricks, such as marked cards and the equipment of the magician. But whoever thinks of fraud here misunderstands the whole situation. The psychical powers of Beulah Miller were not brought before the public by the child or her family; there was no desire for notoriety, [147] and in spite of the very modest circumstances in which this carpenter's family has to live, the facts became known before any commercial possibility suggested itself.

The mother was startled by Beulah's psychical gifts because she noticed two years ago that when the family was playing "Old Maid" Beulah always knew in whose hands the dangerous queen was to be found. Then they began to experiment with cards in the family circle, and her ability to know of what the mother or the sister was thinking became more and more interesting to them. Slowly her school friends began to notice it, and children in the Sunday-school told the minister about Beulah's queer mind-reading. All this time no newspaper had known about it. One day the minister, when he passed the house, entered and inquired whether those rumours were true. He had a little glass full of honey in his pocket, and Beulah spelled the word honey at once. He made some tests with coins, and every one was successful. This minister, Rev. H. W. Watjen, told this to his friend Judge Mason, who has lived in Warren for more than thirty years, and then both the minister and the judge visited repeatedly the village where the Millers live, performed a large number of experiments with cards and coins and words, and [148] became the friendly advisers of the mother, who was still troubled by her doubt whether these supernatural gifts of the child came from God or from the devil. Only through the agency of these two well-known men, the Baptist minister and the judge, was the public informed that a mysterious case existed in the neighbourhood of Warren, and when the newspapers began to send their reporters and strangers came to see the wonder, these two men decided who should see the child. Of course, commercial propositions, invitations to give performances on the vaudeville stage, soon began to pour in, but with indignation the mother refused to listen to any such idea. Because of my scientific interest in such psychological puzzles, the judge and the minister turned to me to investigate the case. It is evident that this whole social situation lacks every conceivable motive for fraud.

But this impression was strongly heightened by the behaviour of the family and of the child during the study which I carried on in the three weeks following. The mother, the twelve-year-old sister Gladys, and Beulah herself were most willing to agree to anything which would make the test difficult, and they themselves asked to have everything tried with no member of the family in the room. Beulah was quite happy to [149] show her art under unaccustomed conditions like having her eyes covered with thick bandages. When inadvertently some one turned a card so that she could see it, she was the first to break out into childish laughter at her having seen it. In short, everything indicated such perfect sincerity, and the most careful examination yielded so absolutely no trace of intentional fraud, that I can vouch for the honesty of the intentions of all concerned in the experiments carried on so far.

If fraud and humbug may certainly be excluded, the wiseacres will say that the results must then have been a matter of chance coincidence. No one can deny that chance may sometimes bring surprising results. Dreams of far-distant accidents come true, and yet no one who considers those millions of dreams which do not come true and which therefore remain disregarded will acknowledge any prophetic power in sleep. It may happen, if you are asked to call a name or a figure of which another man is thinking, that you will strike the right one. Moreover, recent experiments have shown that there is much natural uniformity in the thoughts of men. Certain figures or names or things more readily rush to the mind than others. Hence the chances that two persons will be thinking of the same figure are much larger than would appear from the mere calculation of [150] probabilities. Yet even if we make the largest possible concession to happy coincidences, there cannot remain the slightest doubt that the experiments carried on under standard conditions yielded results the correctness of which endlessly surpasses any possible accidental outcome. We may take a typical illustration: I drew cards which she could not possibly see, while they were shown to the mother and sister sitting next to me, Beulah sitting on the other side of the room. The first was a nine of hearts; she said nine of hearts. The next was six of clubs, to which she said first six of spades; when told it was not spades, she answered clubs. The next was two of diamonds; her first figure was four; when told that it was wrong, she corrected herself two, and added diamonds. The next was nine of clubs, which she gave correctly; seven of spades, she said at first seven of diamonds, then spades; jack of spades, she gave correctly at once, and so on.

One other series: We had little cardboard squares on each of which was a large single letter. I drew any three, put them into the cover of a box, and while the mother, Gladys, and I were looking at the three letters, Beulah, sitting beside us, looked at the ceiling. The first were R-T-O. She said R-T-I. When told it was wrong, she added O. The next were S-U-T; she [151] gave S-U, and then wrongly R P Q, and finally T. The next were N-A-R; she gave G N-A-S R. The following D-W-O she gave D-W, but could not find the last letter. It is evident that every one of the cards gave her fifty-two chances, and not more than one in fifty-two would have been correct if it were only guessing, and as to the letters, not more than one among twenty-six would have been chosen correctly by chance. The given example demonstrates that of five cards she gave three correctly, two half correctly, and those two mistakes were rectified after the first wrong guess. The second experiment demanded from her four times three letters. Of these twelve letters, six were right at the first guess and five after one or two wrong trials. Taking only this little list of card and letter experiments together, we can say that the probabilities are only one to many billions that such a result would ever come by chance.

Yet such correctness was not exceptional. On the contrary, I have no series performed under these conditions which did not yield as favourable an outcome as this. Some were even much more startling. Once she gave six cards in succession correctly. It was no different with word experiments. The printed word at which the sister and I looked was stall; she spelled E S-T-O A-R I L-L. [152] And when the word was steam, she spelled L S-N K T-O A E-A-M; when it was glass, S G-L-R A-S. Whenever a letter was wrong, she was told so and was allowed a second or a third choice, but never more than three. It is evident from these three illustrations that she gave the right letter in the first place six times, and that the right letter was her second choice four times, and her third choice three times, while no letter was missed in three choices. Cases of this type again could never occur by mere chance. The number of successful strokes in this last experiment might be belittled by the claim that the last letters of the word were guessed when the first letters had been found. But this was not the case. First, even such a guess would have been chance. The word might have been grave instead of grass, or star instead of stall. What is much more important, however, is that a large number of other cases proved that she was not aware of the words at all, but spelled the letters without reference to their forming a word. Once I wrote Chicago on a pad. The mother and sister gazed at the word, and Beulah spelled correctly C-H-I-C-A-G, but made eight wrong efforts before she found the closing O. In other cases, she did not notice that the word was completed, and was trying to fish up still other letters from her [153] mind. Everything showed that the word as a word did not come to her mind, but only the single letters. I leave entirely out of consideration the marvels of mind-reading which were secured by the judge and the minister, the male and female newspaper reporters, before I took charge of the study of the case. I rely only on what I saw and of which I took exact notes. I wrote down every wrong letter and every wrong figure, and base my calculation only on this entirely reliable material. Nevertheless, I must acknowledge it as a fact beyond doubt that such results as I got regularly could never possibly have been secured by mere coincidence and chance. As chance and fraud are thus equally out of the question, we are obliged to seek for another explanation.

There is one explanation which offers itself most readily: We saw that in order to succeed, some one around her, preferably the mother and sister, who stand nearest to her heart, have to know the words or the cards. Those visual images must be in some one's mind, and she has the unusual power of being able to read what is in the minds of those others. Such an explanation even seems to some a very modest claim, almost a kind of critical and skeptical view. The judge and the minister, for instance, in accepting this idea of her [154] mind-reading, felt conservative, as through it they disclaimed any belief in mysterious clairvoyance and telepathic powers. In the newspaper stories, where the mysteries grew with the geographical distance from Rhode Island, Beulah was said to be able to tell names or dates or facts which no one present knew. It was asserted that she could give the dates on the coins which any one had in his pocket without the possessor himself knowing them, or that she could give a word in a book on which some one was holding his finger without reading it. No wonder that the public felt sure that she could just as well discover secrets which no one knows and be aware of far-distant happenings. It is only one step from this to the belief in a prophetic foresight of what is to come. For most unthinking people, mind-reading leads in this fashion over to the whole world of mysticism. In sharp contrast to such vagaries, the critical observers like the judge and the minister insisted that there was no trace of such prophetic gifts or of such telepathic wonders to be found, and that everything resolves itself simply into mere mind-reading. Some one in the neighbourhood must have the idea in mind and must fixedly think of it. Only then will it arise in Beulah's consciousness.

But have we really a right to speak of mind-reading [155] itself as if it were such a simple process, perhaps unusual, but not surprising, something like a slightly abnormal state? If we look at it from the standpoint of the scientist, we should say, on the contrary, that there is a very sharp boundary line which separates mind-reading from all the experiences which the scientific psychologist knows. The psychologist has no difficulty in understanding mental diseases like hysteria or abnormal states like hypnotism, or any other unusual variation of mental life. The same principles by which he explains the ordinary life of the mind are sufficient to give account of all the strange and rare occurrences. But when he comes to mind-reading, an entirely new point of view is chosen. It would mean a complete break with everything which science has found in the mental world. The psychologist has never discovered a mental content which was not the effect or the after-effect of the stimulation of the senses. No man born blind has ever by his own powers brought the colour sensations to his mind, and no communication from without was ever traced which was not carried over the path of the senses. The world which is in the mind of my friend, in order to reach my mind, must stimulate his brain, and that brain excitement must lead to the contraction of his mouth muscles, and that must [156] stir the air waves which reach my ear drum, and the excitement must be carried from my ear to the brain, where the mental ideas arise. No abnormal states like hypnotism change in the least this procedure. But if we fancy that the mere mental idea in one man can start the same idea in another, we lack every possible means to connect such a wonder with anything which the scientist so far acknowledges.

To be sure, every sincere scholar devoted to truth has to yield to the actual facts. We cannot stubbornly say that the facts do not exist because they do not harmonize with what is known so far. The psychologist would not necessarily be at the end of his wit if the developments of to-morrow proved that mind-reading in Beulah Miller's case, or in any other case, is a fact beyond doubt. He might argue that all previous knowledge was based on a wrong idea and that, for instance, other processes go on in the brain, which can be transmitted from organism to organism like wireless telegraphic waves without the perception of the senses. If these other processes were conceived as the foundation of mental images, the scientific psychological scholar of the future might possibly work out a consistent theory and all the previously known facts might then be translated into the language of the new science. [157] Whether in this or a similar way we should ever come to really satisfactory results, no one can foresee, but at least it is certain that this would involve a complete giving up of everything which scientists have so far held to be right. Certainly in the history of civilization great revolutions in science have happened. The astronomers had to begin almost anew; why cannot the psychologists turn around and acknowledge that they have been entirely wrong so far and that they must begin once more at the beginning and rewrite all which they have so far taken to be truth?

Certainly the psychologists are no cowards. They would not hesitate to declare their mental bankruptcy if the progress of truth demanded it. But at least we must be entirely clear that this is indeed the situation and that no step on the track of mind-reading can be taken without giving up everything which we have so far held to be true. And it is evident that such a radical break with the whole past of human science can be considered only if every other effort for explanation fails, and if it seems really impossible to understand the facts in the light of all which science has already accomplished. If Beulah Miller's little hands are to set the torch to the whole pile of our knowledge, we ought first to be perfectly sure that there is really nothing [158] worth saving. We cannot accept the theory of the apostles of mind-reading until we know surely that Beulah Miller can receive communications which cannot possibly be explained with the means of science.

Now we all know one kind of mind-reading which looks very astounding and yet which there is no difficulty at all in explaining. It is a favourite performance on the stage, and not seldom tried as a parlour game. I refer to the kind of mind-reading in which one person thinks of a hidden coin, and the other holds his wrist and is then able to find the secreted object. There is no mystery in such apparent transmission of the idea, because it is the result of small unintentional movements of the arm. The one who thinks hard of the corner of the room in which the coin is placed cannot help giving small impulses in that direction. He himself is not aware of these faint movements, but the man who has a fine sense of touch becomes conscious of these motions in the wrist which his fingers grasp, and under the guidance of these slight movements he is led to the particular place. Some persons express their thought of places more easily than others and are therefore better fitted for the game, and we find still greater differences in the sensitiveness of different persons. Not every one can play the game as well as a [159] trained stage performer, who may have an extreme refinement of touch and may notice even the least movements in the wrist which others would not feel at all. Such an explanation is not an arbitrary theory. We can easily show with delicate instruments in the psychological laboratory that every one in thinking of a special direction soon begins to move his hand toward it without knowing anything of these slight movements. The instruments allow the reading of such impulses where the mere feeling of the hand would hardly show any signs. A very neat form of the same type is often seen on the stage when the performer is to read a series of numbers in the mind of some one who thinks intensely of the figures. Some one in the audience thinks of the number fifty-seven. The performer asks him to think of the first figure, then he grasps his hand and counts slowly from zero to nine. After that he asks him to think of the second figure, and counts once more. Immediately after he will announce rightly the two digits. Again there is no mystery in it. He knows that the man who thinks of the figure five will make a slight involuntary movement when the five is reached in counting, and the same movement will occur at the seven in the second counting. If he is very well trained, he will not need the touching of the [160] hand; he will perform the same experiment with figures without any actual contact whatever. It will be sufficient to see the man who is thinking of a figure while he himself is counting. As soon as the dangerous digit is reached, the man will give some unintentional sign. Perhaps his breathing will become a degree deeper, or stop for a moment, his eyelids may make a reflex movement, his fingers may contract a bit. This remains entirely unnoticed by any one in the audience, but the professional mind-reader has heightened his sensibility so much that none of these involuntary signs escapes him. Yet from the standpoint of science his seeing these subtle signs is on principle no different from our ordinary seeing when a man points his finger in some direction.

But the experience of the scientist goes still farther. In the cases of this parlour trick and the stage performance the one who claims to read the mind of the other is more or less clearly aware of those unintended signs. He feels those slight movement impulses, which he follows. But we know from experiences of very different kind that such signs may make an impression on the senses and influence the man, and yet may not really come to consciousness. Even those who play the game of mind-reading in the parlour and who are led by the [161] arm movements to find the hidden coin will often say with perfect sincerity that they do not feel any movements in the wrist which they touch. This is indeed quite possible. Those slight shocks which come to their finger tips reach their brains and control their movements without producing a conscious impression. They are led in the right direction without knowing what is leading them. The physician finds the most extreme cases of such happenings with some types of his hysteric patients. They may not hear what is said to them or see what is shown to them, and yet it makes an impression on them and works on their minds, and they may be able later to bring it to their memory and it may guide their actions, but on account of their disease those impressions do not really reach their conscious minds.

We find the same lack of seeing or hearing or feeling in many cases of hypnotism. But it is not necessary to go to such extreme happenings. All of us can remember experiences when impressions reached our eyes or ears and yet were not noticed at the time, although they guided our actions. We may have been on the street in deep thought or in an interesting conversation so that we were not giving any attention whatever to the way, and yet every step was taken [162] correctly under the guidance of our eyes. We saw the street, although we were not conscious of seeing it. We do not hear a clock ticking in our room when we are working, and yet if the clock suddenly stops we notice it. This indicates that the ticking of the clock reached us somehow and had an effect on us in spite of our not being conscious of it. The scientists are still debating whether it is best to say that these not conscious processes are going on in our subconscious mind or whether they are simply brain processes. For all practical purposes, this makes no difference. We may say that our brain gets an impression through our eyes when we see the street, or through our ears when we hear the clock, or we may say that our subconscious mind receives these messages of eye and ear. In neither case does the scientist find anything mysterious or supernatural.

I am convinced that all the experiences with Beulah Miller may ultimately be understood through those two principles. She has unusual gifts and her performances are extremely interesting, but I think everything can be explained through her subconscious noticing of unintended signs. Where no signs are given which reach her senses, she cannot read any one's mind. But the signs which she receives are not noticed by her consciously. [163] She is not really aware of them; they go to her brain or to her subconscious mind and work from there on her conscious mind.

What speaks in favour of such a skeptical view? I mention at first one fact which was absolutely proved by my experiments—namely, that Beulah Miller's successes turn into complete failures as soon as neither the mother nor the sister is present in the room. All the experiments which I have conducted in which I alone, or I together with the minister and the judge, thought of words or cards or letters or numbers did not yield better results than any one would get by mere guessing. In one series, for instance, in which we all three made the greatest effort to concentrate our minds on written figures, she knew the first number correctly only in two out of fourteen cases. In another series of twelve letters she did not know a single one at the first trial. Sometimes when she showed splendid results with her sister Gladys present, everything stopped the very moment the sister left the room. Sometimes Beulah knew the first half of a word while Gladys stood still in the same room, and could not get the second half of the word when Gladys in the meantime had stepped from the little parlour to the kitchen. Beulah was helpless even when a wooden door was between her [164] and the member of her family. She herself did not know that it made such a difference, but the records leave no doubt. I may at once add here another argument. The good results stop entirely when Beulah is blindfolded. Even when both her mother and sister were sitting quite near her, her mind-reading became pure guesswork when her eyes were covered with a scarf. Again, she liked to make the experiment under this condition and was not aware that her knowledge failed her when she did not see her mother or sister. Her delight in being blindfolded spoke very clearly for her naïve sincerity, but her failure indicated no less clearly that she must be dependent upon unintentional signs for her success.

Let me say at once that some of the observers would probably object to my statement that the presence of the family was needed and that she had to be in such direct connection with them. The newspapers told wonderful stories of her success with strangers, and even the judge and the minister felt certain that they had seen splendid results under most difficult conditions. Yet I have to stick to what I observed myself. It may be objected—and it is well known that this is the pet objection of the spiritualists against the criticism of scholars—that the results come well only when [165] the child is in full sympathy with those present and that I may have disturbed her. But this was not the case. I evidently did not disturb her, inasmuch as we saw that the experiments which I made with her when the sister or the mother was present were most satisfactory. Moreover, she was evidently very much at ease with me when we had become more acquainted, and just those entirely negative results were mostly received on a morning when I had fulfilled the dearest wishes of the two children, a watch for the one and a ring for the other, besides all the candy with which my pockets were regularly stuffed. She was in the happiest frame of mind and most willing to do her best. But if I rely exclusively on my own observation, it is not only because I suppose that the experiments yielded just as good results as those of other observers. It is rather because I know how difficult it is to give reliable accounts from mere memory and to make experiments without long training in experimental methods. All those publicly reported experiments had been made without any actual exact records, and, moreover, by persons who overlooked the most evident sources of error. As a matter of course, I took notes of everything which happened, and treated the case with the same carefulness with which I am accustomed to carry [166] on the experiments in the Harvard Psychological Laboratory.

To give some illustrations of sources of error, I may mention that the earlier observers were convinced that Beulah could not see slight movements of the persons in the room when she was looking fixedly at the ceiling, or that she could not notice the movements of the sister or the mother when she was staring straight into the eyes of the experimenter. Any psychologist, on the contrary, would say that that would be a most favourable condition for watching small signs. He knows that while we fixate a point with the centre of our eye we are most sensitive to slight movement impressions on the side parts of our eye, and that this sensitiveness is often abnormally heightened. Just when the child is looking steadily into our face or to the ceiling, the outside parts of her sensitive retina may bring to her the visible unintentional signs from her sister or mother. The untrained observer is also usually unaware how easily he helps by suggestive movements or utterances to the other observers. When Beulah gave a six instead of a nine, one of our friends whispered that she may have seen it upside down in her mind, or when she gave a zero instead of a six that it looked similar. In short, they keep helping without knowing it. Very [167] characteristic is the habit of unintentionally using phrases which begin with the letters of which they are thinking. The letter in their minds forces them to speak words which begin with it. If they start at a C, we hear "Come, Beulah," if at a T, "Try, Beulah," if at an S, "See, Beulah." It is very hard to protect ourselves against such unintended and unnoticed helps. It is still more difficult to keep the failures in mind. The eager expectancy of hearing the right letter or number from the lips of the child gives such a strong emphasis to the right results that the wrong ones slip from the mind of the hearer. The right figure may be only the third or the fourth guess of the child, but if then the whole admiring chorus around say emphatically at this fourth trial that this is quite right, those three wrong efforts which preceded fade away from the memory. I may acknowledge for myself that I was mostly inclined to believe that the number of the correct answers had been greater than they actually were according to my exact records. For all these reasons I had the very best right to disregard the reports of all those who relied on their amateur art of experimenting and on their mere memory account.

What kind of signs could be in question? It may seem to outsiders that the most wonderful system of [168] signs would be needed for every content of one mind to be communicated to another. But here again we must first reduce the exaggerated claims to the simpler reality. When Beulah makes card experiments, the whole words jack, queen, king, spade, club, heart, diamond, come to her mind, but when she makes word experiments, never under any circumstances does a real word come to her consciousness, but only single letters. Why is this? If king and queen can be transmitted from mind to mind, why not dog and cat? Yet when the mother thinks of dog, it is always only first D, and after a while O, and finally G which creeps into her mind. This difference seems to me most characteristic, because it indicates very clearly that the whole performance is possible only when the communicated content belongs to a small list which can be easily counted. There are only three face cards, only four suites, only ten numbers, and only twenty-six letters, but there are ten thousand words and more. It is easy to connect every one of the ten numbers or every one of the twenty-six letters with a particular sign, but it would be impossible to have a sign for every one of the ten thousand words. Yet if we had to do with real mind-reading, it ought to make no difference whether we transmit the letter D or the word dog. This fact that she can recognize [169] words only by slow spelling, while the faces and the suites of the cards and the names of the numbers come as full words, seems to me to point most clearly to the whole key of the situation. Anything which cannot be brought into such a simple number series, for instance, a colour impression, can never be transmitted. If the mother looks at the ace of diamonds, Beulah says that she sees the red of the diamond before her in her mind, but if the mother looks at the picture of a blue lake, this blue impression can never arise in Beulah's mind, but only the letters B-L-U-E.

Moreover, I observed that for Beulah the letters of the alphabet were indeed connected with numbers, as in seeking a letter she has a habit of going through the alphabet and at the same time moving one finger after another. Thus she feels each letter as having a definite place in her series of finger movements, and the finger movements themselves are often counted by her, so that each letter is finally connected with a special number. This, indeed, reduces the situation to rather a simple scheme. She succeeds only if her mother or sister is present and if her eyes are open, and she succeeds only with material which can be easily counted. A very short system of simple signs would thus be entirely sufficient to communicate everything [170] which her mind-reading brings to her. As to the particular signs, I do not yet feel sure. It would probably take months of careful examination before I should find them out, just as in Germany it has taken months for scholars to discover the unintentional signs which the owner of a trick horse made, from which the horse was apparently able to calculate. I have no time to carry on such an investigation in this case, the more as I do not see that any new insight could be gained by it.

Once I noticed distinctly how in the card experiments the mother without her own knowledge made seven movements with her foot when she thought of the figure seven. That gave me the idea that the signs might be given by very slight knocking on the floor which Beulah's oversensitive skin might notice. What speaks against such a view is that the results stop when she is blindfolded. Yet in this connection I may mention another aspect. It is quite possible that the covering of her eyes may destroy her power, and that nevertheless she may receive her signs chiefly not through the eyes, but through touch and ear. It may be that she needs her eyes open because the seeing of the members of the family may heighten by a kind of autosuggestion her sensitiveness for the perception of the slight signs. I have no doubt that this kind of [171] autosuggestion plays a large rôle in her mind. She can read a card much better when she is allowed to touch with her fingers the rear of the card. She herself believes that she receives the knowledge through her finger tips. In reality it is, of course, a stimulus by which she becomes more suggestible and by which accordingly her sensitiveness to the slight signs which her mother and sister give her becomes increased. We must, however, never forget that these signs, whatever they may be, are not only unintentional on the part of her family, but also not consciously perceived by Beulah. If she stares at the ceiling, and her mother, without knowing it, makes seven slight foot movements, Beulah gets through the side parts of her eye a nerve impression, but she does not think of the foot. This nerve impression, as we saw, works on the subconscious mind, or on the brain, and the idea of seven then arises in her conscious mind like a picture which she can see.

Such a system of signs, completely unknown to those who give them and to her who receives them, cannot have been built up in a short while. But we heard how it originated. At first Beulah recognized the queen in the hands of her sister and mother, when they were playing "Old Maid." There are many who have [172] so much power to recognize the small signs. But when they began to make experiments with cards, probably definite family habits developed; there was much occasion to treat each card individually, to link some involuntary movement with the face cards and some with each suite, and slowly to carry this system over to letters. They all agree that Beulah recognizes some frequent letters much more easily than the rare letters. What the observers have now found was the result of two years' training with mother and sister. Yet all this became possible only because Beulah evidently has this unusual, supernormal sensitiveness together with this abnormal power to receive the signs without their coming at once to consciousness. Her mental makeup in this respect constantly reminds the psychologist of the traits of a hysteric woman.

We have to add only one important point. Some startling results have surely been gained by another method. The same sensitiveness which makes Beulah able to receive signs which others do not notice, evidently makes her able to catch words spoken in a low voice within a certain distance, while she is not consciously giving her attention to them. She picks up bits of conversation which she overhears and which settle in her subconscious mind, until they later come to [173] her consciousness in a way for which she cannot account. All were startled when at the end of our first day together I took a bill in my closed hand and asked her what I had there, and she at once replied a "ten-dollar bill," while they all agreed that the child had never seen a ten-dollar bill before. This result surprised the minister and the judge greatly, and only later did I remember that I had whispered to the judge in the next room, with the door open, that I should ask her to tell the figures on a ten-dollar bill. In the same way the greatest sensation must be explained, which the experiments before my arrival yielded. The New York lady who came with the minister's family and others to the house was overwhelmed when Beulah spelled her name, which, as the affidavit said, was not known to any one else present. This affidavit was as a matter of course given according to the best knowledge of all concerned. Yet when later I came to Warren, one of the participants who told me the incident strengthened it by adding that he was the more surprised when the child spelled the name correctly with a K at the end, as he had understood that it was spelled with a T. In other words, some of those present did know the name, and the lady had evidently either been introduced or addressed by some one, and this had slipped from their minds because [174] Beulah was not in the room. But she was probably in the other room and caught it in her subconscious mind. At her first début before the minister, too, by her same abnormal sensitiveness she probably heard when he told the mother that he had a glass of honey in his pocket. In short, the two actions of her subconscious mind, or of her brain, always go together, her noticing of family signs from her mother and sister and her catching of spoken words from strangers, both under conditions under which ordinary persons would neither see nor hear them. We have therefore nothing mysterious, nothing supernatural before us, but an extremely interesting case of an abnormal mental development, and this unusual power working in a mind which is entirely naïve and sincere.

How long will this naïveté and sincerity last? This is no psychological, but a social problem. Since the newspapers have taken hold of the case, every mail brings heaps of letters from all corners of the country. Some of them bring invitations to give performances, but they are not the most dangerous ones. Most of the letters urge the child to use her mysterious, supernatural powers for trivial or pathetic ends in the interest of the writers. Sometimes she is to locate a lost trunk, or a mislaid pocketbook; sometimes she is to [175] prophesy whether a voyage will go smoothly or whether a business venture will succeed; sometimes she is to read in her mind where a runaway child may be found; and almost always money promises are connected with such requests. The mother, who has not much education but who is a splendid, right-minded country woman with the very best intentions for the true good of her children, has ignored all this silly invasion. She showed me a whole teacupful of two-cent stamps for replies which she had collected from Beulah's correspondence. But I ask again, how long will it last? If Beulah closes her eyes and some chance letters come to her mind, and she forms a word from them and sends it as a reply to the anxious mother who is seeking her child, she will soon discover that it is easy to gather money in a world which wants to be deceived. She is followed by the most tempting invitations to live in metropolitan houses where sensational experiments can be performed with her. The naïve mother is still impressed when a New York woman applies the well-known tricks and assures her that the child reminds her so much of her own little dead niece that she ought to come to her New York house. It is a pity how the community forces sensationalism, commercialism, and finally humbug and fraud on a naïve little country girl who ought [176] to be left alone with her pet lamb in her mother's kitchen. Her gift is extremely interesting to the psychologist, and if it is not misused by those who try to pump spiritualistic superstitions into her little mind or to force automatic writing on her it will be harmless and no cause for hysteric developments. But surely her art is entirely useless for any practical purpose. She cannot know anything which others do not know beforehand. Clairvoyant powers or prophetic gifts are not hers, and above all her mind-reading is a natural process. The edifice of science will not be shaken by the powers of my little Rhode Island friend.

Yet the most important part is not the fate of the individual child, but the behaviour of this nation-wide public which chases her into the swamps of fraud. No one can decide and settle whether the party of superstition forms the majority or the minority. If all the silent voters were sincere, they probably would carry the vote for telepathy. But in any case, such a party exists, and it does not care in the least that scientific [177] investigations clear up a case which threatens to bring our world of thought into chaotic disorder. A world of mental trickery and mystery, a world which by its [178] very principle could never be understood, is to them instinctively more welcome than a world of scientific order. There cannot be a more fundamental contrast [179] between men who are to form a social unit than this radical difference of attitude toward the world of experience. Compared with this deepest split in the community, all its other social questions seem temporary and superficial. [180]

V [181]

THE MIND OF THE JURYMAN

Every lawyer knows some good stories about some wild juries he has known, which made him shiver and doubt whether a dozen laymen ever can see a legal point. But every newspaper reader, too, remembers an abundance of cases in which the decision of the jury startled him by its absurdity. Who does not recall sensational acquittals in which sympathy for the defendant or prejudice against the plaintiff carried away the feelings of the twelve good men and true? For them are the unwritten laws, for them the mingling of justice with race hatreds or with gallantry. And even in the heart of New York a judge recently said to a chauffeur who had killed a child and had been acquitted: "Now go and get drunk again; then this jury will allow you to run over as many children as you like."

Yet whatever the temperament of the jury and its legal insight, we may sharply separate its ideas of deserved punishment from that far more important aspect [182] of its function, the weighing of evidence. The juries may be whimsical in their decisions, they may be lenient in their acquittals or over-rigid in their verdicts of guilty, but that is quite in keeping with the democratic spirit of the institution. The Teutonic nations did not want the abstract law of the scholarly judges; they want the pulse-beat of life throbbing in the court decisions, and what may be a wilful ignoring of the law of the jurists may be a heartfelt expression of the popular sentiment. Better to have some statutes riddled by the illogical verdicts than legal decisions severed from the sense of justice which is living in the soul of the nation. But while a rush into prejudice or a hasty overriding of law may draw attention to some exceptional verdicts, in the overwhelming mass of jury decisions nothing is aimed at but a real clearing up of the facts. The evidence is submitted, and while the lawyers may have wrangled as to what is evidence and what is not, and while they may have tried, by their presentation of the witnesses on their own side and by their cross-examinations, to throw light on some parts of the evidence and shadow on some others, the jurymen are simply to seek the truth when all the evidence has been submitted. And mostly they do not forget that they will live up to their duty best the more they suppress [183] in their own hearts the question whether they like or dislike the truth that comes to light. Whoever weighs the social significance of the jury system ought not to be guided by the few stray cases in which the emotional response obscures the truth, but all praise and blame and every scrutiny of the institution ought to be confined essentially to the ability of the jurymen to live up to their chief responsibility, the sober finding of the true facts.

It cannot be denied that much criticism has been directed against the whole jury system in America as well as in Europe by legal scholars as well as by laymen on account of the prevailing doubt whether the traditional form is really furthering the clearing up of the hidden truth. Where the evidence is so perfectly clear that every one by himself feels from the start exactly like all the others, the coöperation of the twelve men cannot do any harm, but it cannot do any particular good either. Such cases do not demand the special interest of the social reformer. His doubts and fears come up only when difference of opinion exists, and the discussion and the repeated votes overcome the divergence of opinion. The skeptics claim that the system as such may easily be instrumental for suppressing the truth and bringing the erroneous opinion to [184] victory. In earlier times a frequent objection was that lack of higher education made men unfit to weigh correctly the facts in a complicated situation. But this kind of arguing has been given up for a long while. The famous French lawyer who, whenever he had a weak case, made use of his right to challenge jurymen by systematically excluding all persons of higher education, certainly blundered in this respect, according to the views of to-day. Those best informed within and without the legal science agree that the verdicts of straightforward people with public-school education are in the long run neither better nor worse than those of men with college schooling or professional training. A jury of artisans and farmers understands and looks into a mass of neutral material as well as a jury of bankers and doctors, or at least its final verdict has an equal chance to hit the truth.

But the critics say that it is not the lack of general or logical training of the single individual which obstructs the path of justice. The trouble lies rather in the mutual influence of the twelve men. The more persons work together, the less, they say, every single man can reach his highest level. They become a mass with mass consciousness, a kind of crowd in which each one becomes oversuggestible. Each one thinks less reliably, [185] less intelligently, and less impartially than he would by himself alone. We know how men in a crowd do indeed lose some of the best features of their individuality. A crowd may be thrown into a panic, may rush into any foolish, violent action, may lynch and plunder, or a crowd may be stirred to a pitch of enthusiasm, may be roused to heroic deeds or to wonderful generosity, but whether the outcome be wretched or splendid, in any case it is the product of persons who have been entirely changed. In the midst of the panic or in the midst of the heroic enthusiasm no one has kept his own characteristic mental features. The individual no longer judges for himself; he is carried away, his own heart reverberates with the feelings of the whole crowd. The mass consciousness is not an adding up, a mere summation, of the individual minds, but the creation of something entirely new. Such a crowd may be pushed into any paths, chance leaders may use or misuse its increased suggestibility for any ends. No one can foresee whether this heaping up of men will bring good or bad results. Certainly the individual level of the crowd will always be below the level of its best members. And is not a jury necessarily such a group with a mass consciousness of its own? Every individual is melted into the total, has lost his independent [186] power of judging, and becomes influenced through his heightened suggestibility and social feeling by any chance pressure which may push toward error as often as toward truth.

But if such arguments are brought into play, it is evident that it is no longer a legal question, but a psychological one. The psychologist alone deals scientifically with the problem of mutual mental influence and with the reënforcing or awakening of mental energies by social coöperation. He should accordingly investigate the question with his own methods and deal with it from the standpoint of the scientist. This means he is not simply to form an opinion from general vague impressions and to talk about it as about a question of politics, where any man may have his personal idea or fancy, but to discover the facts by definite experiments. The modern student of mental life is accustomed to the methods of the laboratory. He wants to see exact figures by which the essential facts come into sharp relief. But let us understand clearly what such an experiment means. When the psychologist goes to work in his laboratory, his aim is to study those thoughts and emotions and feelings and deeds which move our social world. But his aim is not simply to imitate or to repeat the social scenes of the community. [187] He must simplify them and bring them down to the most elementary situations, in which only the characteristic mental actions are left. Is this not the way in which the experimenters proceed in every field? The physicist or the chemist does not study the great events as they occur in nature on a large scale and with bewildering complexity of conditions, but he brings down every special fact which interests him to a neat, miniature copy on his laboratory table. There he mixes a few chemical solutions in his retorts and his test-tubes, or produces the rays or sparks or currents with his subtle laboratory instruments, and he feels sure that whatever he finds there must hold true everywhere in the gigantic universe. If the waters move in a certain way in the little tank on his table, he knows that they must move according to the same laws in the midst of the ocean. In this spirit the psychologist arranges his experiments too. He does not carry them on in the turmoil of social life, but prepares artificial situations in which the persons will show the laws of mental behaviour. An experiment on memory or attention or imagination or feeling may bring out in a few minutes mental facts which the ordinary observer would discover only if he were to watch the behaviour and life attitudes of the man for years. Everything depends [188] upon the degree with which the characteristic mental states are brought into play under experimental conditions. The great advantage of the experimental method is, here as everywhere, that everything can be varied and changed at will and that the conditions and the effects can be exactly measured.

If we apply these principles to the question of the jury, the task is clear. We want to find out whether the coöperation, the discussion, and the repeated voting of a number of individuals are helping or hindering them in the effort to judge correctly upon a complex situation. We must therefore artificially create a situation which brings into action the judgment, the discussion, and the vote, but if we are loyal to the idea of experimenting we must keep the experiment free from all those features of a real jury deliberation which have nothing to do with the mental action itself. Moreover, it is evident that the situations to be judged must allow a definite knowledge as to the objective truth. The experimenter must know which verdict of his voters corresponds to the real facts. Secondly, the situation must be difficult in order that a real doubt may prevail. If all the voters were on one side from the start, no discussion would be needed. Thirdly, it must be a rather complex situation in order that the judgment [189] may be influenced by a number of motives. Only in this case will it be possible for the discussion to point out factors which the other party may have overlooked, thus giving a chance for changes of mind. All these demands must be fulfilled if the experiment is really to picture the jury function. But it would be utterly superfluous and would make the exact measurement impossible if the material on which the judgment is to be based were of the same kind of which the evidence in the courtroom is composed. The trial by jury in an actual criminal case may involve many picturesque and interesting details, but the mental act of judging is no different when the most trivial objects are chosen.

I settled on the following simple device: I used sheets of dark gray cardboard. On each were pasted white paper dots of different form and in an irregular order. Each card had between ninety-two and a hundred and eight such white dots of different sizes. The task was to compare the number of spots on one card with the number of spots on another. Perhaps I held up a card with a hundred and four dots above, and below one with ninety-eight. Then the subjects of the experiment had to decide whether the upper card had more dots or fewer dots or an equal number compared [190] with the lower one. I made the first set of experiments with eighteen Harvard students. I took more than the twelve men who form a jury in order to reënforce the possible effect, but did not wish to exceed the number greatly, so that the character of the discussion might be similar to that in a jury. A much larger number would have made the discussion too formal or too unruly. The eighteen men sat around a long table and were first allowed to look for half a minute at the two big cards, each forming his judgment independently. Then at a signal every one had to write down whether the number of dots on the upper card was larger, equal, or smaller. Immediately after that they had to indicate by a show of hands how many had voted for each of the three possibilities. After that a discussion began. Indeed, the two cards offered plenty of points for earnest and vivid discussion. During the exchange of opinion in which those who had voted larger tried to convince the party of the smaller, and vice versa, they were always able to look at the cards and to refer to them, pointing to the various parts. One showed how the distances on the one card appeared larger, and another pointed out how the spots were clustered in a certain region, a third how the dots were smaller in some parts, a fourth spoke about the optical illusions, a fifth about [191] certain impressions resulting from the narrowness of the margin, and a sixth about the effect of certain irregularities in the distribution. In short, very different aspects were considered and very different factors emphasized. The discussion was sometimes quite excited, three or four men speaking at the same time. After exactly five minutes of talking the vote was repeated, again at first being written and then being taken by show of hands. A second five minutes' exchange of opinion followed with a new effort to convince the dissenters. After this period the third and last vote was taken. This experiment was carried out with a variety of cards with smaller or larger difference of numbers, but the difference always enough to allow an uncertainty of judgment. Here, indeed, we had repeated all the essential conditions of the jury vote and discussion, and the mental state was characteristically similar to that of the jurymen.

The very full accounts which the participants in the experiment wrote down the following day indicated clearly that we had a true imitation of the mental process in spite of the striking simplicity of our conditions. One man, for instance, described his inner experience as follows: "I think the experiment involves factors quite comparable to those that determine the verdict of [192] a jury. The cards with their spots are the evidence pro and con which each juryman has before him to interpret. Each person's decision on the number is his interpretation of the situation. The arguments, too, seem quite comparable to the arguments of the jury. Both consist in pointing out factors of the situation that have been overlooked and in showing how different interpretations may be possible." Another man writes: "In the experiment it seemed that one man judged by one criterion and another by another, such as distribution, size of spots, vacant spaces, or counting along one edge. Discussion often brought immediate attention to other criterions than those he used in his first judgment, and these often outweighed the original. Similarly, different jurymen would base their opinion on different aspects of the case, and discussion would tend to draw their attention to other aspects. The experiment also illustrated the relative weight given to the opinion of different fellow-jurymen. I found that the statements of a few of the older men who have had more extensive psychological experience weighed more with me than those of the others. Suggestion did not seem to be much of a factor. A man is rather on his mettle, and ready to defend his original impression, until he finds that it is hopeless." Again, another writes: [193] "To me the experiment seemed fairly comparable to the real situation. As in an actual trial, the full truth was not available, but certain evidence was presented to all for interpretation. As to the nature of the discussion itself, I think there was the same mingling of suggestion and real argument that is to be found in a jury discussion." Another says: "The discussion influenced me by suggesting other methods of analysis. For instance, comparison of the amount of open space in two cards, comparison of the number of dots along the edges, estimation in diagonal lines, were methods mentioned in the discussion which I used in forming my own judgments. It does not seem to me that in my own case direct suggestion had any appreciable effect. I was conscious of a tendency toward contrasuggestibility. There was a half submerged feeling that it would be good sport to stick it out for the losing side. The lack of any unusual amount of suggestion and the presence of the influences of analysis and detailed comparison seem to me to show that the tests were in fact fairly comparable to situations in a jury room." To be sure, there were a few who were strongly impressed by the evident differences between the rich material of an actual trial and the meagre content of our tests: there the actions of living men, here the space relations [194] of little spots. But they evidently did not sufficiently realize that the forming of such number judgments was not at all a question of mere perception; that on the contrary many considerations were involved; most men felt the similarity from the start.

What were the results of this first group of experiments? Our interest must evidently be centred on the question of how many judgments were correct at the first vote before any discussion and any show of hands were influencing the minds of the men, and how many were correct at the last vote after the two periods of discussion and after taking cognizance of the two preceding votes. If I sum up all the results, the outcome is that 52 per cent. of the first votes were correct and 78 per cent. of the final votes were correct. The discussion of the successive votes had therefore led to an improvement of 26 per cent. of all votes. Or, as the correct votes were at first 52 per cent., their number is increased by one half. May we not say that this demonstrates in exact figures that the confidence in the jury system is justified? And may it not be added that, in view of the widespread prejudices, the result is almost surprising? Here we had men of high intelligence who were completely able to take account of every possible aspect of the situation. They had time to do so, they [195] had training to do so, and every foregoing experiment ought to have stimulated them to do so in the following ones. Yet their judgment was right in only 52 per cent. of the cases until they heard the opinions of the others and saw how they voted. The mere seeing of the vote, however, cannot have been decisive, because 48 per cent., that is, practically half of the votes, were at first incorrect. The wrong votes might have had as much suggestive influence on those who voted rightly as the right votes on those on the wrong side. If, nevertheless, the change was so strongly in the right direction, the result must clearly have come from the discussion.

But I am not at the end of my story. I made exactly the same experiments also with a class of advanced female university students. When I started, my aim was not to examine the differences of men and women, but only to have ampler material, and I confined my work to students in psychological classes, because I was anxious to get the best possible scientific analysis of the inner experiences. I had no prejudice in favour of or against women as members of the jury, any more than my experiments were guided by a desire to defend or to attack the jury system. I was only anxious to clear up the facts. The women students had exactly the [196] same opportunities for seeing the cards and the votes and for exchanging opinions. The discussions, while carried on for the same length of time, were on the whole less animated. There was less desire to convince and more restraint, but the record, which was taken in shorthand, showed nearly the same variety of arguments which the men had brought forward. Everything agreed exactly with the experiments with the men, and the only difference was in the results. The first vote of all experiments with the women showed a slightly smaller number of right judgments. The women had 45 per cent. correct judgments, as against the 52 per cent. of the men. I should not put any emphasis on this difference. It may be said that the men had more training in scientific observations and the task was therefore slightly easier for them than for most of the women. I should say that, all taken together, men and women showed an equal ability in immediate judgment, as with both groups about half of the first judgments were correct. The fact that with the men 2 per cent. more, with the women 5 per cent. less, than half were right would not mean much. But the situation is entirely different with the second figure. We saw that for the men the discussion secured an increase from 52 per cent. to 78 per cent.; with the women the increase [197] is not a single per cent. The first votes were 45 per cent. right, and the last votes were 45 per cent. right. In other words, they had not learned anything from discussion.

It would not be quite correct if we were to draw from that the conclusion that the women did not change their minds at all. If we examine the number of cases in which in the course of the first, second, and third votes in any of the experiments some change occurred, we find changes in 40 per cent. of all judgments of the men and 19 per cent. of all judgments of the women. This does not mean that a change in a particular case necessarily made the last vote different from the first; we not seldom had a case where, for instance, the first vote was larger, the second equal, and the third again larger. And as a matter of course, where a change between the first and the last occurred, it was not always a change in the right direction. Moreover, it must not be forgotten that the votes always covered three possibilities, and not only two. It was therefore possible for the first vote to be wrong, and then for a change to occur to another wrong vote. The 19 per cent. changes in the decisions of the women contained accordingly as many cases in which right was turned into wrong as in which wrong was turned into right, while with the [198] men the changes to the right had an overweight of 26 per cent. The self-analysis of the women indicated clearly the reason for their mental stubbornness. They heard the arguments, but they were so fully under the autosuggestion of their first decision that they fancied that they had known all that before, and that they had discounted the arguments of their opponents in the first vote. The cobbler has to stick to his last; the psychologist has to be satisfied with analyzing the mental processes, but it is not his concern to mingle in politics. He must leave it to others to decide whether it will really be a gain if the jury box is filled with individuals whose minds are unable to profit from discussion and who return to their first idea, however much is argued from the other side. It is evident that this tendency of the female mind must be advantageous for many social purposes.

The woman remains loyal to her instinctive opinion. Hence we have no right to say that the one type of mind is in general better than the other. We may say only that they are different, and that this difference makes the men fit and the women unfit for the particular task which society requires from the jurymen.

Practical experience seems to affirm this experimental result on many sides. The public of the east is still too [199] little aware of this new and yet powerful influence in the far west, where the jury box is accessible to women. There is no need to point to extreme cases. Any average trial may illustrate the situation. I have before me the reports of the latest murder trial at Seattle, the case of Peter Miller. The case was unusual only in that the defendant had been studying criminal law during his incarceration in jail, and addressed the jury himself on his own behalf in an argument that is said to have lasted nine hours. The jury was out quite a long time. Eleven were for acquittal, one woman was against it. The next day the papers brought out long interviews with her in which she explained the situation. She characterized her general standing in this way: "I am a dressmaker, and go out every day, six days in the week. I read the classified ads and glance at the headlines, but I don't have much time to waste on anything else." But her attitude in the jury room was very similar. She says: "I was sure of my opinion. I didn't try to change anybody else's opinion. I just kept my own. They argued a good deal and asked me if the fact that eleven of twelve had been convinced by the same evidence of Peter Miller's innocence didn't shake my faith in my own judgment. Well, it didn't. We were out twenty-four hours. I borrowed a pair of [200] knitting needles from one of the jurors, and I sat there and knitted most of the time." The State of Washington will now have to have a new trial, as the jury could not agree. There will probably still be many hung juries because some dressmaker borrows a pair of knitting needles from one of the jurors, knits most of the time, and lets the others argue, as she is sure of her own opinion. The naïve epigram of this model juror, "I didn't try to change anybody else's opinion; I just kept my own," illuminates the whole situation. This is no contrast to the popular idea that woman easily changes her mind. She changes it, but others cannot change it.

In order to make quite sure that the discussion and not the seeing of the vote is responsible for the marked improvement in the case of men, I carried on some further experiments in which the voting alone was involved. To bring this mental process to strongest expression, I went far beyond the small circle which was needed for the informal exchange of opinion, and operated instead with my large class of psychological students in Harvard. I have there four hundred and sixty students, and accordingly had to use much larger cards with large dots. I showed to them any two cards twice. There was an interval of twenty seconds between the first and the second exposures, and each [201] time they looked at the cards for three seconds. In one half of the experiments that interval was not filled at all; in the other half a quick show of hands was arranged so that every one could see how many on the first impression judged the upper card as having more or an equal number or fewer dots than the lower. After the second exposure every one had to write down his final result. The pairs of cards which were exposed when the show of hands was made were the same as those which were shown without any one knowing how the other men judged. We calculated the results on the basis of four hundred reports. They showed that the total number of right judgments in the cases without showing hands was 60 per cent. correct; in those with show of hands about 65 per cent. A hundred and twenty men had turned from the right to the wrong—that is, had more incorrect judgments when they saw how the other men voted than when they were left to themselves.

It is true that those who turned from worse to better by seeing the vote of the others were in a slight majority, bringing the total vote 5 per cent. upward, but this difference is so small that it could just as well be explained by the mere fact that this act of public voting reënforced the attention and improved a little the total [202] vote through this stimulation of the social consciousness. It is not surprising that the mere seeing of the votes in such cases has such a small effect, incomparable with that of a real discussion in which new vistas are opened, inasmuch as in 40 per cent. of the cases the majority was evidently on the wrong side from the start. Those who are swept away by the majority would therefore in 40 per cent. of the cases be carried to the wrong side. I went still further and examined by psychological methods the degree of suggestibility of those four hundred participants in the experiment, and the results showed that the fifty most suggestible men profited from the seeing of the vote of the majority no more than the fifty least suggestible ones. In both cases there was an increase of about 5 per cent. correct judgments. I drew also from this the conclusion that the show of hands was ineffective as a direct influence toward correctness, and that it had only the slight indirect [203] value of forcing the men to concentrate their attention better on those cards. All results, therefore, point in the same direction: it is really the argument which brings a coöperating group nearer to the truth, and not the seeing how the other men vote. Hence [204] the psychologist has every reason to be satisfied with the jury system as long as the women are kept out of it.

VI [205]

EFFICIENCY ON THE FARM

We city people who are feeding on city-made public opinion forget that we are in the minority, and that the interests of the fifty millions of the rural population are fundamental for the welfare of the whole nation. Moreover, the life of the city itself is most intimately intertwined with the work on the farm; banking and railroading, industrial enterprises and commercial life, are dependent upon the farmers' credit and the farmers' prosperity. The nation is beginning to understand that it would be a calamity indeed if the tempting attractiveness of the city should drain off still more the human material from the village and from the field. The cry "back to the land" goes through the whole world, and this means more than a camping tour in the holidays and some magazine numbers of *Country Life in America* by the fireplace. Its meaning ought to be that every nation which wants to remain healthy and strong must take care that the obvious advantages of metropolitan life [206] are balanced by the joys and gains of the villager who lacks the shop windows and the exciting turmoil.

Certainly the devices of the city inventor, the telephone and the motor car and a thousand other gifts of the last generation, have overcome much of the loneliness, and the persistent efforts of the states to secure better roads and better schools in the country have enriched and multiplied the values of rural life. Yet the most direct aid is, after all, that which increases the efficiency of farming itself. In this respect, too, we feel the rapid progress throughout the country. The improvements in method which the scientific efforts of all nations have secured are eagerly distributed to the remotest corners. The agents of the governmental Bureau of Agriculture, the agricultural county demonstrators, the rapidly spreading agricultural schools, take care that the farmer's "common-sense" with its backwardness and narrowness be replaced by an insight which results from scientific experiment and exact calculation. Agricultural science, based on physics and chemistry, on botany and zoölogy, has made wonderful strides during the last few decades. It must be confessed that the self-complaisance of the farmer and the power of tradition have offered not a little resistance to the practical application of the knowledge [207] which the agricultural experiments establish, and the blending of the well-known conservative attitude of the farmer with a certain carelessness and deficiency in education has kept the production of the American farm still far below the yielding power which the present status of knowledge would allow. Other nations, more trained in hard labour and painstaking economy and accustomed to most careful rotation of crops, obtain a much richer harvest from the acre, even where the nature of the soil is poor. But the longing of the farmer for the best methods is rapidly growing, too, and in many a state he shows a splendid eagerness to try new ways, to develop new plans, and to progress with the advance of science.

In such an age it seems fair to ask whether the circle of sciences which are made contributory to the efficiency of the agriculturist has been drawn large enough. It is, of course, most important for every farmer to know the soil and whatever may grow on it and feed on it. All the new discoveries as to the power of phosphates to increase the crop or as to the part which protozoa play in the inhibition of fertility, or the influence of parasites on the enemies of the crops and the numberless naturalistic details of this type, are certainly most important. Yet does it not look as if in all the operations which the [208] worker on the land has to perform everything is carefully considered by science, and only the chief thing left out, the worker and his work? He is earnestly advised as to every detail in the order of nature: he learns by what chemical substances to improve the soil, what seeds are to be used, and when they are to be planted, what breeds of animals to raise and how to feed them. But no scientific interest has thrown light on his own activity in planting the seed and gathering the harvest, in picking the fruit and caring for the stock.

No doubt, the agent of some trust has recommended to him the newest machines; but their help still belongs, after all, to the part of outer nature. They are physical apparatus, and even if the farmer uses nowadays dynamite to loosen the soil, all this new-fashioned power yet remains scientific usage of the knowledge of nature. But behind all this physical and chemical material in which and through which the farmer and his men are working stand the farmer himself with his intelligence, and his men themselves with their lack of intelligence. This human factor, this bundle of ideas and volitions and feelings and judgments, must ultimately be the centre of the whole process. There is no machine which can do its best if it is wrongly used, no tool which can be effective if it is not set to work by [209] an industrious will. The human mind has to keep in motion that whole great mechanism of farm life. It is the farmer's foresight and insight which plough and plant and fill the barns. For a long while the average farmer thought about nature, too, that he could know all he needed, if he applied his home-made knowledge. That time has passed, and even he relies on the meteorology telegram of the scientific bureaus rather than on the weather rules of his grandfather. But when it comes to the mental processes which enter into the agricultural work, he would think it queer to consult science. He would not even be aware that there is anything to know. The soil and the seed and even the plough and the harvester are objects about which you can learn. But the attention with which the man is to do his work, the memory, the perception, the ideas which make themselves felt, the emotions and the will which control the whole work, would never be objects about which he would seek new knowledge; they are no problems for him, they are taken for granted.

Yet we have to-day a full-fledged science which does deal with these mental processes. Psychology speaks about real things as much as chemistry, and the laws of mental life may be relied on now more safely than the laws of meteorology. It seems unnatural that those [210] who have the interests of agriculture at heart should turn the attention of the farmer exclusively to the results of the material sciences and ignore completely the thorough, scientific interest in the processes of the mind. To be sure, until recently we had the same shortcoming in industrial enterprises of the factories. Manufacturer and workingman looked as if hypnotized at the machines, forgetting that those wheels of steel were not the only working powers under the factory roof. A tremendous effort was devoted to the study and improvement of the industrial apparatus and of the raw material, while the mental fitness and the mental method of the army of workingmen was dealt with unscientifically and high-handedly. But within the last few years the attention of the industrial world has been seriously turned to the matter-of-course fact that the workman's mind is more important than the machine and the material, if the highest economic output is to be secured. The great movement for scientific management, however much or little its original plans may survive, has certainly once for all convinced the world that the study of the man and his functions ought to be the chief interest of the market, even in our electrical age; and the more modest movement for vocational guidance has emphasized this personal factor from sociological [211] motives. At last the psychologists themselves approached the problem of the worker in the factory, began to examine his individual fitness for his work, and to devise tests in order to select quickly those whose inborn mental capacity makes them particularly adjusted to special lines of work. Above all, they examined the methods by which the individual learned and got his training in the technical activities, they began to determine the exact conditions which secured the greatest amount of the best possible work with the greatest saving of human energy. All this is certainly still at its beginning, but even if the solutions of the problems are still insufficient, the problems themselves will not again be lost sight of. The most obvious acknowledgment of the importance of these demands lies in the fact that already the quack advice of pseudo-psychologists is offered from many sides. The up-to-date manufacturer knows, even if he is not interested in the social duties involved, that the mere economic interest demands a much more serious study of the workingman's mind than any one thought of ten years ago.

This change must finally come into the agricultural circles. The consequences of the usual, or rather invariable neglect, are felt less in agriculture than in [212] industry, because the work is so much more scattered. The harmful effects of poor adjustment and improper training must be noticed more easily where many thousands are crowded together within the walls of the same mill. But it would be an illusion to fancy that the damage and the loss of efficiency are therefore less in the open field than in the narrow factory. On the contrary, the conditions favour the workshop. There everybody stands under constant supervision, and what is still more important, always has the chance for imitation. Every improvement, almost every new trick and every new hand movement which succeeds with one, is taken up by his neighbour and spreads over the establishment. The principle of farm work is isolation. One hardly knows what another is doing, and where several do coöperate, they are generally engaged in different functions. Even where the farmhands work in large groups, the attitude is much less that of team work than of a mere summation of individual workers. In the country as a whole the man who works on the farm has to gather his experience for himself, has to secure every advance for himself, and has to miss the benefit which the social atmosphere of industrial work everywhere furnishes.

It would be utterly misleading to think that the long [213] history of mankind's agricultural pursuits ought to have been sufficient to bring together the necessary experience. The analysis of the vocational activities has given every evidence that even the oldest functions are performed in an impractical, inefficient way. The students of scientific management have demonstrated how the work of the mason, as old as civilization itself, is carried on every day in every land with methods which can be improved at once, as soon as a scientific study of the motions themselves is started. It could hardly be otherwise, and the principle might be illustrated by any chance case. If a girl were left to herself to learn typewriting, the best way would seem to her to be to pick out the letters with her two forefingers. She would slowly seek the right key for each letter and press it down. In this way she would be in the pleasant position of producing a little letter after only half an hour of trial. As soon as she has succeeded with such a first half page, she will see only the one goal of increasing the rapidity and accuracy, and by hard training she will indeed gain steadily in speed and correctness, and after a year she will write rather quickly. Yet she will never succeed in reaching the ideal proficiency. In order to attain the highest point, she ought to have started with an entirely different method. [214] She ought to have begun at once to use all her fingers, and, moreover, to use them without looking at the keyboard. If she had started with this difficult method she would never have succeeded in writing a letter the first day. It would have taken weeks to reach that achievement which the simpler method yields almost at once. But in plodding along on this harder road she would finally outdistance the competitor with the commonsense method and would finally gain the highest degree of efficiency. This is exactly the situation everywhere. Commonsense always grasps for those methods which quickly lead to a modest success, but which can never lead to maximum achievement. On the other hand, up to the days of modern experimental psychology the interest was not focussed on the mental operations involved in industrial life as such. Everything was left to commonsense, and therefore it is not surprising that the farmhand like the workingman in the mill has never hit upon the one method which is best, as all his instincts and natural tendencies had to lead him to the second or third best method, since these alone give immediate results.

A highly educated man who spent his youth in a corn-raising community reports to me the following psychological observation: However industrious all [215] the boys of the village were, one of them was always able to husk about a half as much more corn than any one else. He seemed to have an unusual talent for handling so many more ears than any one of his rivals could manage. Once my friend had a chance to inquire of the man with the marvellous skill how he succeeded in outdoing them so completely, and then he learned that no talent was involved, but a simple psychological device, almost a trick. The worker who husks the ear is naturally accustomed to make his hand and finger movements while his eyes are fixed on them. As soon as one ear is husked, the attention turns to the next, the eyes look around and find the one which best offers itself to be handled next. When the mind, under the control of the eyes, has made its choice, the mental impulse is given to the arms, and the hands take hold of it. Yet it is evident that these manipulations can be carried on just as well without the constant supervision of the eyes. The eye is needed only to find the corn and to direct the impulse of the hands toward picking it up. But the eye is no longer necessary for the detailed movements in husking. Hence it must be possible to perform that act of vision and that choice of the second ear while the hands are still working on the first. The initial stage of the work [216] on the second ear then overlaps the final stages of the work with the first, and this must mean a considerable saving of time.

This was exactly the scheme on which that marvel of the village had struck. He had forced on himself this artificial breaking of the attention, and had trained himself to have his eyes performing their work independent of the activity of the hands. My friend assures me that as soon as he had heard of the trick, there was no difficulty in his imitating it, and immediately the number of ears which he was able to husk in a given time was increased by 30 per cent. The mere immediate instinct would always keep the eye movement and the hand movements coupled together. A certain artificial effort is necessary to overcome this natural coördination. But if this secret scheme had been known to all the boys in the village, ten would have been able to perform what fifteen did. Of course this is an utterly trivial incident, and where my friend husked corn in his boyhood days, to-day probably the cornharvester is doing it more quickly anyhow. But as long as real scientific effort has not been applied toward examining the details, we have to rely on such occasional observations in order at first to establish the principle. Every one knows that just such illustrations [217] might as well be taken from the picking of berries, in which the natural method is probably an absurd waste of energy, and yet which in itself seems so insignificant that up to present days no scientific efforts have been made to find out the ideal methods.

Similar accidental observations are suggested by the well-known experiments with shovelling carried on in the interest of industry, where the shovelling of coal and of pig iron demanded a careful investigation into the best conditions for using the shovel. It was found that it is an unreasonable waste of energy to use the same size and form of tool for lifting the heavy and the light material. With the same size of shovel the iron will make such a heavy load that the energies are exhausted, and the coal will give such a light load that the energies are not sufficiently made use of. It became necessary to determine the ideal load with which the greatest amount of work with the slightest fatigue could be performed, and that demanded a much larger shovel for the light than for the heavy substance. Exactly this situation repeats itself with the spade of the farmer. The conditions are somewhat different, but the principle must be the same. Of course the farmer may use spades of different sizes, but he is far from bringing the product of spade surface and weight to a definite [218] equation. Sometimes he wastes his energies and sometimes he exhausts them. But it is not only a question of the size of shovel or spade. The whole position of the body, the position of the hands, the direction of the attention, the rhythm of the movement, the pauses between the successive actions, the optical judgment as to the place where the spade ought to cut the ground, the distribution of energy, the respiration, and many similar parts of the total psychophysical process demand exact analysis if the greatest efficiency is to be reached. Everybody knows what an amount of attention the golf player has to give to every detail of his movement, and yet it would be easier to discover by haphazard methods the best way to handle the golf stick than to use the spade to the best effect.

On the other hand, the better method is not at all necessarily the more difficult one. More effort is needed at the beginning to acquire an exactly adjusted scheme of movement, but as soon as the well-organized activity has become habitual, it will realize itself with less inner interference. For the educated it is no harder to speak correct grammar than to speak slang, and it is no more difficult to write orthographically than to indulge in chaotic spelling, just as in every field it is no harder to show good manners than to behave rudely. [219] If the sciences of digging and chopping, of reaping and raking, of weeding and mowing, of spraying and feeding, are all postulates of the future, each can transform the chance methods into exact ones, and that means into truly efficient ones, only when every element has been brought under the scrutiny of the psychological laboratory. We must measure the time in hundredths of a second, must study the psychophysical conditions of every movement, where not trees are cut or hay raked, but where the tools move systems of levers which record graphically the exact amount and character of every partial effect. The one problem of the distribution of work and rest alone is of such tremendous importance for the agricultural work that a real scientific study of the details might lead to just as much saving as the introduction of new machinery. The farmhand, who would never think of wasting his money, wastes his energies by contracting big muscles, where a better economized system of movement would allow him to reach the same result through the contraction of smaller muscles, which involves much less energy and much less fatigue. The loss by wrong bending and wrong coördination of movement may be greater than by bad weather.

Yet commonsense can never be sufficient to find the [220] right motor will impulses. The ideal distribution of pauses is extremely different from merely stopping the work when a state of overfatigue has been reached. Even general scientific rules could not be the last word. Subtle psychological tests would have to be devised by which the plan for alternation between work and rest could be carefully adjusted to the individual needs of every rural worker. The mere sensation of fatigue may be entirely misleading. It must be brought into definite relations to temperature, moistness, character of the work, training, and other factors. On the other hand, the absence of fatigue feeling would be in itself no indication that the limit of safety has not been passed, and yet the work itself must suffer when objective overfatigue of the system has begun. At the right moment a short interruption may secure again the complete conditions for successful work. If that moment has passed, an exhaustion may result which can no longer be repaired by a short rest. Any wrong method of performing these simple activities, that is, any method which is not based on exact scientific analysis, wastes the energies of the workingman, and by that the economic means of the farm owner, and indirectly the economic resources of the whole nation. In the Harvard Psychological Laboratory we are at present engaged [221] in the investigation of such an apparently trivial function as sewing by hand. The finger which guides the needle is attached to a system of levers which write an exact graphic record of every stitch on a revolving drum. And the deeper we enter into this study the more we discover that such a movement, of which every seamstress and every girl who makes her clothes feels that she knows everything, contains an abundance of important features of which we do not as yet know anything. With the same scientific exactitude the laboratory must investigate the milking, or the making of butter, the feeding of the cattle and the picking of the fruit, the use of the scythe and the axe, the pruning and the husking. The mere fact that every one, even with the least skill, is able to carry out such movements with some result, does not in the least guarantee that any one carries them out today with the best result possible.

The governmental experiment station ought to establish regular psychological laboratories, in which the mental processes involved in the farmer's activity would be examined with the same loyalty to modern science with which the chemical questions of the soil or the biological questions of the parasites are furthered. Only such investigations could give the right cues also [222] to the manufacturers of farming implements. At present the machines are constructed with the single purpose of greatest physical usefulness, and the farmer who uses them has to adjust himself to them. The only human factor which enters into the construction so far has been a certain desire for comfort and ease of handling. But as soon as the mental facts involved are really examined, they ought to become decisive for the details of the machine. The handle which controls the lever, and every other part, must be placed so that the will finds the smallest possible resistance, so that one psychical impulse prepares the way for the next, and then a maximum of activity can be reached with the smallest possible psychophysical energy. Such a psychological department of the agricultural station could be expanded, and study not only the mental conditions of farming, but examine also the psychological factors which belong indirectly to the sphere of agricultural work. It may examine the mental effects which the various products of the farm stir up in the customers. The feelings and emotions, the volitions and ideas which are suggested by the vegetables and fruits, the animals and the flowers, are not without importance for the success in the market. The psychology of colour and taste, of smell and touch and [223] form, may be useful knowledge for the scientific farmer, and even his methods of packing and preparing for the market, of displaying and advertising, may be greatly improved by contact with applied psychology.

At least one of the psychological side problems demands especial attention, the mental life of the animals. Animal psychology is no longer made up of hunting stories and queer observations on ants and wasps, and gossip about pet cats and dogs and canary birds. It has become an exact science, which is housed in the psychological laboratories of the universities. And with this change the centre of interest has shifted, too. The mind of the animals is not studied in order to satisfy our zoölogical interest, but really to serve an understanding of the mental functions. It was therefore appropriate to introduce those methods which had been tested in human psychology. In our Harvard Psychological Laboratory, in which a whole floor of the building is devoted exclusively to animal experiments under specialists, single functions like memory or attention or emotion are tested in earthworms or turtles or pigeons or monkeys, and the results are no less accurate than those of subtlest human work. But this experimental animal psychology has so far served theoretical interests only. It stands where human psychology [224] stood before the contact with pedagogy, medicine, law, commerce, and industry suggested particular formulations of the experiments. Such contact with the needs of practical life ought to be secured now for animal psychology. The farmer who has to do with cows and swine and sheep, with dogs and horses, with chickens and geese, with pigeons and bees, ought to have an immediate interest to seek this contact. But his concern ought to go still further. He has to fight the animals that threaten his harvest.

The farmer himself knows quite well how important the psychical behaviour of the animals is for his success. He knows how the milk of the cows is influenced by emotional excitement, and how the handling of horses demands an understanding of their mental dispositions and temperaments. Sometimes he even works already with primitive psychological methods. He makes use of the mental instinct which draws insects to the light when he attracts the dangerous moths with light at night in order to destroy them. Ultimately all the traps and nets with which the enemies of the crop are caught are schemes for which psychotechnical calculations are decisive. The means for breaking the horses, down to the whip and the spur and the blinders, are after all the tools of applied psychology. The manufacturer [225] is already beginning to supply the farmer with some practical psychology: dogs which despise the ordinary dog biscuits, seem quite satisfied with the same cheap foods when they are manufactured in the form of bones. The dog first plays with them and then eats them. There is no reason why everything should be left to mere tradition and chance in a field in which the methods are sufficiently developed to give exact practical results, as soon as distinct practical questions are raised. There would be no difficulty in measuring the reaction times of the horses in thousandths of a second for optical and acoustical and tactual impressions, or in studying the influence of artificial colour effects on the various insects in the service of agriculture.

Especial importance may be attached to those investigations in animal psychology which trace the inheritance of individual characteristics. The laboratory psychologist studies, for instance, the laws according to which qualities like savageness and tameness are distributed in the succeeding generations. He studies the proportions of those traits in hundreds of mice, which are especially fit for the experiment on account of their quick multiplication. But this may lead immediately to important results for the farmers with reference to mental traits in breeding animals. It [226] would be misleading if it were denied that all this is a programme to-day and not a realization, a promise and not a fulfilment. The field is practically still uncultivated. But in a time in which the nation is anxious to economize the national resources, which were too long wasted, and in which the need of helping the farmer and of intensifying the values of rural life is felt so generally, it would be reckless to ignore a promise the fulfilment of which seems so near. To be sure, the farmers cultivated their fields through thousands of [227] years without chemistry, just as they do their daily work to-day without psychology, but nobody doubts that the introduction of scientific chemistry into farming has brought the most valuable help to the national, and to the world economy. The time seems really ripe for experimental psychology to play the same rôle for the benefit of mankind, which in the future as in the past will [228] always be prosperous only when the farmer succeeds.

VII [229]

SOCIAL SINS IN ADVERTISING

There is one industry in the world which may be called, more than any other, a socializing factor in our modern life. The industry of advertising binds men together and tightly knits the members of society into one compact mass. Every one in the big market-place of civilization has his demands and has some supply. But in order to link supply and demand, the offering must be known. The industry which overcomes the isolation of man with his wishes and with his wares lays the real foundation of the social structure. It is not surprising that it has taken gigantic dimensions and that uncounted millions are turning the wheels of the advertising factory. The influence and civilizing power of the means of propaganda go far beyond the help in the direct exchange of goods. The advertiser makes the modern newspaper and magazine possible. These mightiest agencies of public opinion and intellectual culture are supported, and their technical perfection [230] secured, by those who pay their business tax in the form of advertisements.

Under these circumstances it would appear natural to have just as much interest and energy and incessant thought devoted to this very great and significant industry as to any branch of manufacturing. But the opposite is true. Armies of engineers and of scientifically trained workers have put half a century of scholarly research and experimental investigation into the perfecting of the physical and chemical industries.

The most thorough study is devoted to the raw material and to the machines, to the functions of the workingman and to everything which improves the mechanical output. In striking contrast to this, the gigantic industry of advertising is to-day still controlled essentially by an amateurish impressionism, by a so-called commonsense, which is nothing but the uncritical following of a well-worn path. Surely there is an abundance of clever advertisement writers at work, and great establishments make some careful tests before they throw their millions of circulars before the public. Yet even their so-called tests have in no way scientific character. They are simply based on watching the success in practical life, and the success is gained by instinct. Commonsense tells even the most superficial advertiser [231] that a large announcement will pay more than a small one, an advertisement in a paper with a large circulation more than in a paper with a few subscribers, one with a humorous or emotional or exciting text more than one with a tiresome and stale text. He also knows that the cover page in a magazine is worth more than the inner pages, that a picture draws attention, that a repeated insertion helps better than a lonely one. Yet even a score of such rules would not remove the scheme of advertising from the commonplaces of the trade. They still would not show any trace of the fact that the methods of exact measurement and of laboratory research can be applied to such problems of human society.

Advertising is an appeal to the attention, to the memory, to the feeling, to the impulses of the reader. Every printed line of advertisement is thus a lever which is constructed to put some mental mechanism in motion. The science of the mental machinery is psychology, which works on principles with the exact methods of the experiment. It seems unprogressive, indeed, if just this one industry neglects the help which experimental science may furnish. A few slight beginnings, to be sure, have been made, but not by the men of affairs, whose practical interests are involved. They [232] have been made by psychologists who in these days of carrying psychology into practical life have pushed the laboratory method into the field of advertising.

The beginnings indicated at once that much which is sanctioned by the traditions of economic life will have to be fundamentally revised. Psychologists, for instance, examined the memory value of the different parts of the page. Little booklets were arranged in which words were placed in the four quarter pages. The advertiser is accustomed patiently to pay an equal amount for his quarter page, whether it is on the left half or the right, on the lower or on the upper part of the page. The experiment demonstrated that the words on the upper right-hand quarter had about twice the memory value of those on the lower left. The advertiser who is accustomed to spend for his insertion on the lower left the same sum as for that on the upper right throws half his expenditure away. He reaches only half of the customers, or takes only half a grasp of those whom he reaches. This case, which can be easily demonstrated by careful experiments, is typical of the tremendous waste which goes on in the budget of the advertising community. And yet the advertiser would not like to act like the poet who sings his song not caring whose heart he will stir. [233]

As long as the psychologist is only aware of an inexcusable waste of means by lack of careful research into the psychological reactions of the reader, he may leave the matter to the business circles which have to suffer by their carelessness. But this economic wrong may coincide with cultural values in other fields, and the social significance of the problem may thus become accentuated. A problem of this double import, economic and cultural at the same time, to-day faces publishers, advertisers, and readers. It is of recent origin, but it has grown so rapidly and taken such important dimensions that at present it overshadows all other debatable questions in the realm of propaganda. The movement to which we refer is the innovation of mixing reading matter and advertisements on the same page. In the good old times a monthly magazine like *McClure's* or the *American* or the *Metropolitan* or the *Cosmopolitan* showed an arrangement which allowed a double interpretation. One interpretation, the idealistic one, was that the magazine consisted of articles and stories in solid unity, which formed the bulk of the issue. In front of this content, and after it, pages with advertisements were attached. The other interpretation, which suggested itself to the less ambitious reader, was that the magazine consisted of a heap of entertaining [234] advertisement pages, between which the reading matter was sandwiched. But in any case there was nowhere mutual interference. The articles stood alone, and the automobiles, crackers, cameras, and other wares stood alone, too. All this has been completely changed in the last two or three years. With a few remarkable exceptions like the *Atlantic Monthly*, the *World's Work*, and the *Century*, the overwhelming majority of the monthly and weekly papers have gone over to a system by which the tail of the stories and articles winds itself through the advertisement pages, and all the advertising sheets are riddled by stray pieces of reading matter. The immediate purpose is of course evident. If the last dramatic part of the story suddenly stops on page 15 and is continued on page 76, between the announcements of breakfast food and a new garter, the publisher, or rather the advertiser, hopes, and the publisher does not dare to contradict, that some of the emotional interest and excitement will flow over from the loving pair to the advertised articles. The innocent reader is skilfully to be guided into the advertiser's paradise.

We claimed that here the economic innovation, whether profitable or not, has its cultural significance. The sociologists who have thought seriously about the [235] American type of civilization have practically agreed in the conviction that the shortcoming of the American mind lies in its lack of desire for harmony and unity. It is an æsthetic deficiency which counts not only where art and artificial beauty are in question, but shows still more in the practical surroundings and the forms of life. The nation which is and always has been controlled by strong idealistic moral impulses takes small care of the æsthetic ideals. The large expenditures for external beautification must not deceive. Just as the theatre is to the American essentially entertainment and amusement and fashion, but least of all a life need for great art, so on the whole background of daily life a thousand motives show themselves more effectively than the longing for inner unity and beautiful fitness. The masses who waste their incomes for beautiful clothes, not because they are beautiful, but because they are demanded by the fashion, patiently tolerate the dirt in the streets, the crowding of cars, the chewing of gum, the vulgar slang in speech, and shirt-sleeve manners. But this undeveloped state of the sense of inner harmony has effects far beyond the mere outer appearances. The hysterical excitement in politics, the traditional indifference to corruption and crime up to the point where they become intolerable, the bewildering [236] mixture of highest desire for education and cheapest faith in superstitions and mysticism and quacks, all must result from a social mind in which the æsthetic demand for harmony and proportion is insufficiently developed. The one great need of the land is a systematic cultivation of this æsthetic spirit of unity. It cannot be forced on the millions by any sudden and radical procedures. The steady, cumulating influences of the whole atmosphere of civic life must lead to a slow but persistent change. Fortunately, many such helpful agencies are at work. Not only the systematic moulding of the child's mind by art instruction, and of the citizen's mind by beautiful public buildings, but a thousand features of the day aid in bringing charm and melody to the average man.

Seen from this point of view the new fashion in the makeup of the periodical literature is a barbaric and inexcusable interference with the process of æsthetic education. A page on which advertisements and reading matter are mixed is a mess which irritates and hurts a mind of fine æsthetic sensitiveness, but which in the uncultivated mind must ruin any budding desire for subtler harmony. The noises of the street, with all the whistles of the factories and the horns of the motor cars, are bad enough, and the anti-noise crusade is quite [237] in order. Yet the destructive influence of those chaotic sounds is far weaker than the shrillness and restlessness of these modern specimens of so-called literature. The mind is tossed up and down and is torn hither and thither, following now a column of text while the advertisements are pushing in from both sides, and then reading the latest advertisement while the serious text is drawing the attention. It is the quantity which counts. The popular magazines which circulate in a million copies and reach two or three million minds are the loudest preachers of this sermon of bewilderment and scramble. A consciousness on which these tumultuous pages hammer day by day must lose the subtler sense of proportionate harmony and must develop an instinctive desire for harshness and crudeness and chaos. To overcome this riot of the printing press is thus a truly cultural task, and yet it is evident that the mere appeal to the cultural instinct will not change anything as long as the publisher and, above all, the advertiser, are convinced that they would have to sacrifice their personal profit in the interest of æsthetic education. If an end is to be hoped for, it can be expected only if it is discovered that the calculation of profit is erroneous, too. But this is after all a question of naked facts, and only the scientific examination can decide. [238]

The problem might be approached from various sides. It was only meant as a first effort when I carried on the following experiment: I had a portfolio with twenty-four large bristol-board cards of the size of the *Saturday Evening Post*. On eight of those cards I had pasted four different advertisements, each filling a fourth of a page. On some pages every one of the four advertisements took one of four whole columns; in other cases the page was divided into an upper and lower, right and left part. All the advertisements were cut from magazines, and in all the name of the firm and the object to be sold could be easily recognized. On the sixteen other pages the arrangement was different. There only two fourths of the page were filled by two advertisements; the other two fourths contained funny pictures with a few words below. These pictures were cut from comic papers. All the pictures were of such a kind that they slightly attracted the attention by their amusing content or by the cleverness of the drawing, but never demanded any careful inspection or any delay by the reading of the text. This, in most cases, consisted of a few title words like "The Widow's Might," "Pause, father, is that whip sterilized?" or similar easily grasped descriptions of the story in the picture. Even where the text took two lines, it was more easy [239] to apperceive the picture and its description than the essentials of the often rather chaotic advertisements. By this arrangement we evidently had thirty-two advertisements on the eight pages which contained nothing else, and thirty-two other advertisements on the sixteen pages which contained half propaganda and half pictures with text. All this material was used as a basis for the following test, in which forty-seven adult persons participated. All were members of advanced psychological courses, partly men, partly women. None of those engaged in the experiment knew anything about the purpose beforehand. Thus they had no theories, and I carefully avoided any suggestion which might have drawn the attention in one or another direction.

Every one had to go through those twenty-four pages in twelve minutes, devoting exactly thirty seconds to every page, and a signal marked the time when he had to pass to the next. He was to give his attention to the whole content of the page, and as both the pictures and the advertisements were chosen with reference to their being easily understood and quickly grasped, an average time of more than seven seconds for each of the four offerings on the page was ample, even for the slow reader. Of course the time would not have been sufficient to read every detail in the advertisements, [240] but no one had any interest in doing so, as they were instructed beforehand to keep in mind essentially the advertised article and the firm, and in the case of the pictures a general impression of the idea.

As soon as the twenty-four pages had been seen, every one was asked to write down the ideas of five of the funny pictures within three minutes. The results of this were of no consequence, as the purpose was only to fill the interval of the three minutes in order that all the memory pictures of the advertisements might settle down in the mind and that all might have an equal chance If we had turned immediately to the writing down of firms and articles, the last ones seen would have had an undue advantage. But when the three minutes had been filled with an effort to remember some of the funny pictures and to write down their salient points, all the mental after-images of the pages had faded away, and a true memory picture was to be produced. In the presentation care was taken to have the twenty-four pages follow in irregular order, the pages of straight advertising mixed with those of the double content. After the three minutes every one had to write down as many names of firms with the articles as his memory could reproduce. The time was now unlimited. Nothing else was to be added; the reference to the particular advertisement [241] was entirely confined to the firm and the object. Where they knew the firm name without the object, or the article without the advertiser, they had to make a dash to indicate the omission. The aim was to discover whether the thirty-two advertisements on the mixed pages had equal chances in the mind with the thirty-two on the straight advertisement pages. In order to have an exact basis of comparison, we counted every name 1, and every article 1. Thus when firm and object were correctly given it was counted 2.

Of course there were very great individual differences. It is evident that a person who would have remembered all the sixty-four advertisements on this basis of calculation would have made 128 points. The maximum which was actually made was in the case of two women, each of whom reached 50 points. One man reached 49. The lowest limit was touched in the exceptional case of one woman who made only 11 points. The average was 28.4. These figures seem small, considering that less than a fourth were kept in mind, and even by the best memory less than a half, but it must be considered that in the modern style of advertisement the memory is burdened with many side features of the announcement, and that the result is therefore smaller than if name and article had been memorized in an isolated [242] form. But these figures have no relation to our real problem. We wanted to compare the memory fate of the advertisements on the one kind of pages with that of the parallel advertisements on the other kind. As soon as we separate the two kinds of reproduced material we find as total result that the forty-seven persons summed up 570 points for the advertisements on pages with comic pictures, but 771 for the advertisements on pages which contained nothing else. The average individual thus remembered about six whole advertisements out of the thirty-two on the combined pages, and about eight and a fifth of the thirty-two on the straight pages. Among the forty-seven persons, there were thirty-six who remembered the straight-page notices distinctly better than the mixed-page advertisements, and only eleven of the forty-seven showed a slight advantage in favour of the mixed pages. In the case of the men this difference is distinctly greater than in the case of the women. Only two of the fifteen men who participated showed better reproducing power for the mixed material, while nine of the thirty-two women favoured it. As the advertiser is not interested in the chance variations and exceptional cases among the reading public, but naturally must rely on the averages, the results show clearly that the propaganda made on [243] pages which do not contain anything but advertisements has more than a third greater chances, as the relation was that of 6 to 8.2.

The result is hardly surprising. We recognized that the conditions for the apprehension of the special advertisements are in themselves equally favourable for both groups. As the pictures were very easily grasped, it may even be said that there was more time left for the study of the advertisements on the mixed pages, and yet the experiment showed that they had a distinct disadvantage. The self-observation of the experimenters leaves hardly any doubt that the cause for this lies in the different attitude which the mixed pages demand from the reader. The mental setting with which those pictures or the written matter is observed, is fundamentally different from that which those propaganda notices demand. If the mind is adjusted to the pleasure of reading for its information and enjoyment, it is not prepared for the fullest apprehension of an advertisement as such. The attention for the notice on the same page remains shallow as long as the entirely different kind of text reaches the side parts of the eye. On those pages, on the other hand, which contain announcements only, a uniform setting of the mind prepared the way for their fullest effectiveness. [244] The average reader who glances over the pages of the magazines is not clearly aware of these psychological conditions, and yet that feeling of irritation which results from the mixing of reading matter and propaganda on the same page is a clear symptom of this mental reaction. The mere fact that both the advertisements and stories or anecdotes or pictures are seen in black and white by the retina of the eye, and are in the same way producing the ideas of words and forms in the mind, does not involve the real psychological effect being the same. The identical words read as a matter of information in an instructive text, and read as an argument to the customer in a piece of propaganda, set entirely different mental mechanisms in motion. The picture of a girl seen with the understanding that it is the actress of the latest success, or seen with the understanding that it is an advertisement for a toilet preparation, starts in the whole psychophysical system different kinds of activities, which mutually inhibit each other. If we anticipate the one form of inner reaction, we make ourselves unfit for the opposite.

An interesting light falls on the situation from experiments which have recently been carried on by a Swedish psychologist. He showed that in every learning process the intention with which we absorb the memory [245] material is decisive for the firmness with which it sticks to our mind. If a boy learns one group of names or figures or verses with the intention to keep them in mind forever, and learns another group of the same kind of material with the same effort and by the same method, but with the intention to have them present for a certain test the next day, the mental effect is very different. Immediately after the learning, or on the morning of the next day, he has both groups equally firmly in his mind, but three days later most of what was learned to be kept is still present. On the other hand, those verses and dates which were learned with the consciousness that they had to serve the next day have essentially faded away when the time of the test has passed, even if the test itself was not given. Every lawyer knows from his experience how easily he forgets the details of the case which has once been settled by the court, as he has absorbed the material only for the purpose of having it present up to the end of the procedure. These Swedish experiments have given a cue to further investigations, and everything seems to confirm this view. It brings out in a very significant way that the impressions which are made on our mind from without are in their effectiveness on the mind entirely dependent upon the subjective attitude, and the idea [246] that the same visual stimuli stir up the same mental reactions is entirely misleading. The attitude of reading and the attitude of looking at advertisements are so fundamentally different that the whole mental mechanism is in a different setting.

The result is that whenever we are in the reading attitude, we cannot take the real advertising effect out of the pictures and notices which are to draw us to the consumption of special articles. The editor who forces his wisdom into the propaganda page is hurting the advertiser, who, after all, pays for nothing else but the opportunity to make a certain psychological impression on the reader. He gets a third more of this effect for which he has to pay so highly if he can have his advertisement on a clean sheet which brings the whole mind into that willing attitude to receive suggestions for buying only. It is most probable that the particular form of the experiment here reported makes this difference between advertising pages with and without reading matter much smaller than it is in the actual perusal of magazines, as we forced the attention of the individual on every page for an equal time. In the leisurely method of going through the magazine the interfering effect of the editorial part would be still greater. Compared with this antagonism of mental setting, it means [247] rather little that these scattered pieces of text induce the reader to open the advertisement. If we were really of that austere intellect which consistently sticks to that which is editorially backed, we should ignore the advertisements, even if they were crowded into the same page. They might reach our eye, but they would not touch our mind. Yet there is hardly any fear that the average American reader will indulge in such severity of taste. He is quite willing to yield to the temptation of the advertising gossip with its minimum requirement of intellectual energy for its consumption. He will therefore just as readily turn from the articles to the advertisements if they are separated into two distinct parts. Frequent observations in the Pullman cars suggested to me rather early the belief that these advertisement parts in the front and the rear of the magazine were the preferred regions between the two covers.

Just as the great public habitually prefers the light comedy and operetta to the theatre performances of high æsthetic intent, it moves instinctively to those printed pages on which a slight appeal to the imagination is made without any claim on serious thought. It is indeed a pleasant tickling of the imagination, this leisurely enjoyment of looking over all those picturesque [248] announcements; it is like passing along the street with its shopwindows in all their lustre and glamour. But this soft and inane pleasure has been crushed by the arrangement after to-day's fashion. Those pages on which advertising and articles are mixed helterskelter do not allow the undisturbed mood. It is as if we constantly had to alternate between lazy strolling and energetic running. Thus the chances are that the old attractiveness of the traditional advertising part has disappeared. While those broken ends of the articles may lead the reader unwillingly to the advertisement pages, he will no longer feel tempted by his own instincts to seek those regions of restlessness; and if he is of more subtle sensitiveness, the irritation may take the stronger form, and he may throw away the whole magazine, advertisement and text together. The final outcome, then, must be disadvantageous to publisher and advertiser alike. The publisher and the editor have certainly never yielded to this craving of the advertiser for a place on the reading page without a feeling of revolt. Commercialism has forced them to submit and to make their orderly issues places of disorder and chaos. The advertisers have rushed into this scheme without a suspicion that it is a trap. The experiments have proved that they are simply injuring [249] themselves. As soon as this is widely recognized, a countermovement ought to start. We ought again to have the treasures of our magazines divided into a [250] straight editorial and a clean advertisement part. The advertisers will profit from it in dollars and cents through the much greater psychological effectiveness of [251] their announcements, the editors will be the gainers by being able to present a harmonious, sympathetic, restful magazine, and the great public will be blessed by the removal of one of the most malicious nerve irritants [252] and persistent destroyers of mental unity.

VIII [253]

THE MIND OF THE INVESTOR

The psychologist who tries to disentangle the interplay of human motives finds hardly a problem for his art to solve when he approaches the conscientious investor. His work has brought him savings, and his savings are to work for him. Hence they must not lie idle, and in the complicated market, with its chaotic offerings, he knows what he has to do. He seeks the advice of the expert, and under this guidance, he buys that which combines great safety with a fair income. The intellectual and emotional processes which here take control of the will and of the decision are perfectly clear and simple, and the mental analysis offers not the least difficulty. The fundamental instincts of man on the background of modern economic conditions must lead to such rational and recommendable behaviour. A psychological problem appears only when such a course of wisdom is abandoned, and either the savings are hidden away instead of being made productive, or [254] are thrown away in wildcat schemes. Yet of the two extremes the first again is easily understood. A hysteric fear of possible loss, an unreasonable distrust of banks and bankers, keeps the overcautious away from the market. But while such a state of mind is said to be frequent in countries in which the economic life is disorderly, enterprising Americans seldom suffer from this ailment, and even the theoretical doctrine that it is sinful to have capital working seems not to have affected practically those who have the capital at their disposal. The specific American case is the opposite one, and with regard to those reckless investors it seems less clear what psychological conditions lie at the bottom of their rashness.

Foreign visitors have indeed often noticed with surprise that the American public, in spite of its cleverness and its practical trend and its commercial instinct, is more ready to throw its money into speculative abysses than the people of other lands. What is the reason? Those observers from abroad are usually satisfied with the natural answer that the Americans are gamblers, or that they have an indomitable desire for capturing money without working. But the students of comparative sociology cannot forget the fact that many national institutions and customs of other lands suggest [255] that the blame might with much more justice be directed against the other party. America prohibits lotteries, while lotteries are flourishing on the European continent. The Austrians, Italians, and Spaniards are slaves to lotteries, and even in sober Germany the state carries on a big lottery enterprise. President Eliot once said in a speech about the moral progress of mankind that a hundred years ago a public lottery was allowed in Boston for the purpose of getting the funds for erecting a new Harvard dormitory, and he added that such a procedure would be unthinkable in New England in our more enlightened days. Yet in the most civilized European countries, whenever a cathedral is to be built, or an exhibition to be supported, the state gladly sanctions big lottery schemes to secure the financial means. The European governments argue that a certain amount of gambling instinct is ingrained in human character, and that it is wiser to create a kind of official outlet by which it is held within narrow limits, and by which the results yielded are used for the public good.

This may be a right or a wrong policy, but in any case, it shows that the desire for gambling is no less marked on the other side of the ocean. In the same way, while private bookmakers are not allowed at most European races, the official "totalisators" offer to the [256] gamblers the same outlets. Every tourist remembers from the European casinos in the summer resorts the famous game with the little horses, a miniature Monaco scheme. And in the privacy of the too often not very private clubs extremely neat card games are in order which depend still more upon chance than the American poker. Moreover, the Europeans have not even the right to say that American life indicates a desire for harvest without ploughing. Every observer of European life knows to what a high degree the young Frenchman or Austrian, Italian, German, or Russian approaches married life with an eye on the dowry. Hundreds of thousands consider it as their chief chance to come to ease and comfort. The whole temper of the nations is adjusted to this idea, which is essentially lacking in American society. It is evident that no method of getting rich quick is more direct, and from a higher point of view more immoral, if taken as a motive for the choice of a mate, than this plan which Europe welcomes. The same difference shows itself in smaller traits. Europe invented the tipping system, which also means that money is expected without an equivalent in labour. Tipping is essentially strange to the American character, however rapid its progress has been on the Atlantic seaboard. [257]

Of course it would be absurd to ignore the existence and even the prevalence of similar attitudes in America. If the dowry does not exist, not every man marries without a thought of the rich father-in-law. Forbidden gambling houses are abundant, private betting connected with sport is flourishing everywhere; above all, the economic organization admits through a back-door what is banished from the main entrance, by allowing stocks to be issued for very small amounts. In Germany the state does not permit stocks smaller than one thousand marks, equal to two hundred and fifty dollars, with the very purpose of making speculative stock buying impossible for the man of small means. The waiter and the barber who here may buy very small blocks of ten-dollar stocks have no such chance there. Stock buying is thus confined to those circles from which a certain wider outlook may be expected. The external framework of the stock market is here far more likely to tempt the man of small savings into the game, and the mere fact that this form has been demanded by public consciousness suggests that the spirit which craves lotteries is surely not absent in the new world, even though the lottery lists in the European newspapers are blackened over before they are laid out in the American public libraries. A certain [258] desire for gambling and quick returns evidently exists the world over. But if the Americans are really speculating more than all the other nations, a number of other mental features must contribute to the outcome.

One tendency stands quite near to gambling, and yet is characteristically different, the delight in running risks, the joy in playing with dangers. Some races, in which the gambling instinct is strong, are yet afraid of high risks, and the pleasure in seeking dangerous situations may prevail without any longing for the rewards of the gambler. It seems doubtful whether this adventurous longing for unusual risks belongs to the Anglo-Saxon mind. At least those vocations which most often involve such a mental trend are much more favoured by the Irish. It is claimed that they, for instance, are prominent among the railroad men, and that the excessive number of accidents in the railroad service results from just this reckless disposition of the Irishmen. It tempts them to escape injury and death only by a hair. Where this desire to feel the nearness of danger, yet in the hope of escaping it, meets the craving for the excitement of possible gain, a hazardous investment of one's savings must be expected.

Yet it would be very one-sided and misleading if this group of emotional features were alone made responsible [259] for the lamentable recklessness in the market. We must first of all necessarily acknowledge the tremendous powers of suggestion which the whole American life and especially the stock market contains. The word suggestion has become rather colourless in popular language, but for the psychologist, it has a very definite meaning. Suggestion is always a proposition for action, which is forced on the mind in such a way that the impulse to opposite action becomes inhibited. Under ordinary circumstances, when a proposition is made to do a certain thing through the mechanism of the mind, the idea of the opposite action may arise. If some one tells the normal man to go and do this or that, he will at once think of the consequences, and in his mind perhaps the idea awakes of the dangerousness or of the foolishness, of the immorality or of the uselessness of such a deed, and any one of these ideas would be a sufficient motive for ignoring the proposed line of behaviour and for suppressing the desire to follow the poor advice. But often this normal appearance of the opposite ideas fails. If they arise at all, they are too faint or too powerless to offer resistance, and often they may not even enter consciousness. They remain suppressed, and the result is that the idea of action finds its way unhindered, and breaks out into the deed which [260] normally would have been checked. If this is the case, the psychologist says that the mind was in a state of increased suggestibility.

The degree of suggestibility, that is of willingness to yield to such propositions for action and of inability to resist them, is indeed different from man to man. We all know the stubborn persons who are always inclined to resist whatever is proposed to them and who do not believe what is told them, and we know the credulous ones who believe everything that they see printed. But the degree of suggestibility changes no less from hour to hour with the individual. In a state of fatigue or under the influence of alcohol or under the influence of strong emotions, in hope and fear, the suggestibility is reënforced. The highest degree of suggestibility is that mental state which we call hypnotism, in which the power to resist the proposed idea of action is reduced to a minimum. But the chief factor in making us suggestible is the method by which the idea of action is proposed, and in psychology we speak of suggestion whenever an action is proposed by methods which make the mind yielding. It certainly is not objectionable to exert suggestive influence. Suggestions are the leading factors in education, in art, and in religion. The authoritative voice with which the [261] teacher proposes the right thing has a most valuable suggestive power to suppress in the child the opposite misleading impulse. But surely suggestions can become dangerous and destructive. If actions are proposed in a form which paralyzes the power to become conscious of the opposite impulses, the voice of reason and of conscience is silenced, and social and moral ruin must be the result.

Everybody at once thinks of the endless variety of advertisements. An announcement which merely gives information is of course no suggestion. But if perhaps such an announcement takes the form of an imperative, an element of suggestion creeps in. To be sure we are accustomed to this trivial pattern, and no one completely loses his power to resist if the proposition to buy comes in the grammatical form of a command. If we had reached the highest degree of suggestibility, as in hypnotism, we could not read "Cook with gas" without at once putting a gas stove into our kitchen. Yet even such a mild suggestion has its influence and tends slightly to weaken the arguments which would lead to an opposite action. The advertisements, however, which the brokers send to our house and which are spread broadcast in the homes of the country to people who have no technical knowledge [262] of stock-buying are surely not confined to such child-like and bland forms of suggestion. The whole grouping of figures, the distribution of black and white in the picture of the market situation, the glowing story of the probable successes with the bewildering hints of special privileges, must increase the suggestibility of the untrained mind and reënforce powerfully the suggestive energy of the proposition to buy. The whole technique of this procedure has nowhere been brought to such virtuosity as in our country. The fact which we mentioned, that the new industrial and mining enterprises can offer shares small enough to be accessible to the man without means, has evidently been the chief reason for developing a style of appeal which would be unthinkable in the countries where the investors are essentially experienced business men.

But the skill of the prospectus with its sometimes half fraudulent features would, after all, not gain such influence if suggestion were not produced from another side as well, namely, through the instinct of imitation. The habit of making risky investments is so extremely widespread that the individual buyer does not feel himself isolated, and therefore dependent upon his own judgments and deliberations. He feels himself as a member of a class, and the class easily becomes a crowd, [263] even a mob, a mob in which the logic of any mob reigns, and that is the logic of doing unthinkingly what others do. It is well known that every member of a crowd stands intellectually and morally on a lower level than he would stand if left to his spontaneous impulses and his own reflections. The crowd may fall into a panic and rush blindly in any direction into which any one may have happened to start and no one thinks about it, or it may go into exaltation and exuberantly do what no one alone would dare to risk. This mass consciousness is also surely a form of increased suggestibility. The individual feels his own responsibility reduced because he relies instinctively on the judgment of his neighbours, and with this decreased responsibility the energy for resistance to dangerous propositions disappears. Men buy their stocks because others are doing it.

But finally, may we not call it suggestion, too, if the individual even tremblingly accepts the risks of perilous deals, because he feels obliged to grasp for an unusually high income in order to live up to the style of his set? Of course there is no objective standard of living if we abstract from that where the income simply secures the needs of bare existence. Above that, everything depends upon the habits of those around us. If [264] the community steadily screws up these habits, makes life ostentatious for those of moderate means as well as for the rich, hysterically emphasizes the material values, the will to be satisfied with the income of safe investments has to fight against tremendous odds. The truly strong mind will keep its power to resist, but the slightly weak mind will find the suggestion of the surrounding life more powerful than the fear of possible loss. If all the neighbours in the village have automobiles, the man who would enjoy a quiet book and a pleasant walk much more than a showy ride will yield, and spend a thousand dollars for his motor car where fifty dollars for books would have brought him far more intense satisfaction. In no country have fashion and ostentatiousness taken such strong possession of the masses, and the willingness to be satisfied with a moderate income is therefore nowhere so little at home.

Yet neither gambling and taking risks, nor suggestibility and imitation, are the whole of the story. We must not forget the superficiality of thinking, the uncritical, loose, and flabby use of the reasoning power which shows itself in so many spheres of American mass life. It is sufficient to see the triviality of argument and the cheapness of thought in those newspapers which seek and enjoy the widest circulation. It is difficult [265] not to believe that fundamentally sins of education are to blame for it. The school may bring much to the children, but no mere information can be a substitute for a training in thorough thinking. Here lies the greatest defect of our average schools. The looseness of the spelling and figuring draws its consequences. Whoever becomes accustomed to inaccuracy in the elements remains inaccurate in his thinking his life long. If the American public loses a hundred million dollars a year by investments in worthless undertakings, surely not the smallest cause is the lack of concise reasoning. Wrong analogies control the thought of the masses. Any copper stock must be worth buying because the stock of Calumet-Hecla multiplied its value a hundredfold. But the irony of the situation lies in the fact that, as experience shows, those who are the clearest thinkers in their own fields are in the realm of investments as easily trapped as the most superficial reasoners. It is well known that college professors, school teachers, and ministers figure prominently on the mailing lists of unscrupulous brokers, and their hard-earned savings are especially often given for stocks which soon are not worth the paper on which they are printed. Sometimes, to be sure, this unpractical behaviour of the idealists really results from an unreasonable indifference [266] to commercial questions. The true scholar, whose life is tuned to the conviction that he has more important things to do in the world than to make money, readily falls into a mood of carelessness with regard to the money which he does chance to make. In this state of indifference he follows any advice and may easily be misled.

But it seems probable that the more frequent case is the opposite one. Just because the teacher and the pastor have small chance to save anything, they give their fullest thought to the question how to multiply their earnings, and their mistake springs rather from their ignorance of the actual conditions. They think that they can figure it out by mere logic and overlook the hard realities. They resemble another group of victims who can be found in the midst of commercial life, the over-clever people who rely on especially artificial arguments. They feel sure that they see some points which no one else has discovered, and while they may have noticed some small reasonable points, they overlook important conditions which the simpler-minded would have seen. They know everything better than their neighbours, and whatever their friends buy or sell they at once have a brilliant argument to prove that the step was wrong. They generally forget that the listener [267] must be suspicious of their wisdom, as they themselves have never earned the fruit of their apparent wisdom. They all, however, may find comfort in the well-known fact that hardly any great financier has died, not even a Harriman or a Morgan, without there being found in his possession large quantities of worthless stocks and bonds. But the variety of intellectual types, the careless and the uncritical, the over-clever and the illogical thinkers, could easily protect themselves against the dangers of the shortcomings in their mental mechanism if their minds had not another trait, which, too, is more frequent in America than anywhere else in the world—the lack of respect for the expert.

The average American is his own expert in every field. This is certainly not a reproach. It supplies American public life with an immense amount of energy and readiness to help. Above all, historically, it was the necessary outcome of the political democracy. In striking contrast to the European bureaucracy, any citizen could at any time be called to be postmaster or mayor or governor or member of the cabinet. A true American would find his way, however complex the work before him. That was, and is, splendid. Yet the development of the recent decades has clearly [268] shown that the danger of this mental attitude after all appears to the newer American generation alarmingly great in many fields. Civil service has steadily grown, the influence of the engineer and the expert in every technical and practical field has more and more taken control of American life, because the go-as-you-please methods of the amateur have shown increasingly their ineffectiveness. Education has slowly been removed from the dilettantic, unprepared school boards. The reign of the expert in public life seems to have begun. But in private life such an attitude is still a part of the mental equipment of millions. They ignore the physician and cure themselves with patent medicines or mental healing; they ignore the banker and broker and make their investments in accordance with their own amateurish inspiration. They pick up a few data, ask a few friends who are as little informed as themselves, but do not think of asking the only group of men who make a serious, persistent study of the market their lifework.

They call this independence, and it cannot be denied that some features of our home and school education may have fostered this tendency not to submit to the judgment of those who know better. They have grown up in schools in which the kindergarten method [269] never stopped, in which they were permitted to select the studies which they liked, and to learn just what pleased them; they were brought up in homes in which they were begged and persuaded, but never forced to do the unwelcome; in short, they have never learned to submit their will to authority. It cannot be surprising that they fancy that it is the right kind of mental setting to feel one's self the ultimate authority in every field, and it would be harmless indeed if the patent [270] medicines would really cure as well as the prescriptions of the physician, and if the wildcat schemes would really yield the same safe income as those investments recommended by the reliable banker. It is then, after all, no chance that this commercially clever American [271] nation wastes more in anti-economic fancies than any other people on the globe. It is the outcome of psychological traits which are rooted in significant conditions of our educational and social life. Yet as soon as these connections are recognized and these reasons for waste are understood, it ought not to be difficult [272] fundamentally to change all this and to make the savings of the nation everywhere really sources of national income.

IX [273]

SOCIETY AND THE DANCE

The story of the dance is the history of human civilization, of its progress and regress. To be sure, as the human mind remains ultimately the same, mankind has often unintentionally returned again to the old forms. The pirouette, which the artists of the ballet invented a hundred years ago, and which was applauded as the wonder of its time, as we now know, was danced by old Egyptians. Not seldom the same outer forms referred to very different mental motives. We learn that many people danced half naked as an expression of humility. Who would claim that the lack of costume in the ballet of to-day is a symbol of humility, too? Moreover, the right perspective can hardly be gained as long as we take the narrow view and think only of those few forms of dance which we saw yesterday in the ballroom and the day before yesterday on the stage of the theatre. The dance has not meant to mankind only social pleasure and artistic spectacle, [274] it originally accompanied the social life and surrounded the individual in every important function.

Dancing certainly began as a religious cult. It was the form in which every increase of emotion expressed itself, grief as well as joy, awe as much as enthusiasm. The primitive peoples danced and in many places still dance when the seasons change or when the fields are to be cultivated, when they start on the hunt or go to war, when health is asked for the sick, and when the gods are to be called upon. The Iroquois Indians have thirty-two chief types of dances, and even among civilized nations, for instance the Bohemians, a hundred and thirty-six dances may be discriminated. Moreover, at first, the dance is really one with the song; music and dancing were only slowly torn asunder. And if we look over the whole world of dance, it almost appears as if what is left to us is after all merely a poor remnant. Yet in these very days much seems to suggest that the dance is to come to its own again. At least, he who observes the life along Broadway may indeed suspect that dancing is now to be intertwined again with every business of life, and surely with every meal of life. No longer can any hostelry in New York be found without dancing, and wider still than the dance sweeps the discussion about it. The dance seems once [275] more the centre of public interest; it is cultivated from luncheon to breakfast; it is debated in every newspaper and every pulpit.

But is not all this merely a new demonstration that the story of the dance is the story of civilization? Can we deny that this recent craze which, like a dancing mania, has whirled over the country, is a significant expression of deep cultural changes which have come to America? Only ten years ago such a dancing fever would have been impossible. People danced, but they did not take it seriously. It was set off from life and not allowed to penetrate it. It had still essentially the rôle which belonged to it in a puritanic, hardworking society. But the last decade has rapidly swept away that New England temper which was so averse to the sensuous enjoyment of life, and which long kept an invisible control over the spirit of the whole nation. Symptoms of the change abound: how it came about is another question. Certainly the increase and the wide distribution of wealth with its comforts and luxuries were responsible, as well as the practical completion of the pioneer days of the people, the rich blossoming of science and art, and above all the tremendous influx of warm-blooded, sensual peoples who came in millions from southern and eastern Europe, and who [276] altered the tendencies of the cool-blooded, Teutonic races in the land. They have changed the old American Sunday, they have revolutionized the inner life, they have brought the operas to every large city, and the kinemetograph to every village, and have at last played the music to a nation-wide dance. Yet the problem which faces every one is not how this dancing craze arose, but rather where it may lead, how far it is healthy and how far unsound, how far we ought to yield to it or further it, and how far we ought to resist. To answer this question, it is not enough to watch the outside spectacle, but we must inquire into the mental motives and mental consequences. Exactly this is our true problem.

Let us first examine the psychological debit account. No one can doubt that true dangers are near wherever the dancing habit is prominent. The dance is a bodily movement which aims at no practical purpose and is thus not bound by outer necessities. It is simply self-expression: and this gives to the dancing impulse the liberty which easily becomes licentiousness. Two mental conditions help in that direction; the mere movement as such produces increased excitement, and the excitement reënforces the movement, and so the dance has in itself the tendency to become quicker and wilder [277] and more and more unrestrained. When gay Vienna began its waltzing craze in the last century, it waltzed to the charming melodies of Lanner in a rhythm which did not demand more than about one hundred and sixty movements in a minute; but soon came Johann Strauss the father, and the average waltzing rhythm was two hundred and thirty a minute, and finally the king of the waltz, Johann Strauss the younger, and Vienna danced at the rhythm of three hundred movements. But another mental effect is still more significant than the impulse to increase rapidity. The uniformity of the movements, and especially of the revolving movement, produces a state of half dizziness and half numbness with ecstatic elements. We know the almost hypnotic state of the whirling dervishes and the raptures in the savage war dances; all this in milder form is involved in every passionate dance. But nothing is more characteristic of such half-hypnotic states than that the individual loses control of his will. He behaves like a drunken man who becomes the slave of his excitement and of every suggestion from without. No doubt many seek the dancing excitement as a kind of substitute for the alcoholic exaltation.

The social injury which must be feared if the social community indulges in such habits of undisciplined, [278] passionate expression needs no explaining. The mind is a unit: it cannot be without self-control in one department and under the desirable self-discipline of the will in another. A period in which the mad rush of dancing stirs social life must be unfavourable to the development of thorough training and earnest endeavour. The fate of imperial Rome ought to be the eternal warning to imperial Manhattan. Italy, like America, took its art and science from over the sea, but gave to them abundant wealth. Instead of true art, it cultivated the virtuosi, and in Rome, which paid three thousand dancers, the dance was its glory until it began ingloriously to sink.

Not without inner relation to the inebriety, and yet distinctly different, is the erotic character of the dance. Lovemaking is the most central, underlying motive of all the mimic dances all over the globe. Among many primitive peoples the dance is a real pantomimic presentation of the whole story from the first tender awaking of a sweet desire through the warmer and warmer courtship to the raptures of sensual delight. Civilized society has more or less covered the naked passion, but from the graceful play of the minuet to the graceless movements of the turkey trot the sensual, not to say the sexual, element can easily be recognized [279] by the sociologist. Here again cause and effect move in a circle. Love excitement expresses itself in dance, and the dance heightens the love excitement. This erotic appeal to the senses is the chief reason why the church has generally taken a hostile attitude. For a long while the dance was denounced as irreligious and sinful on account of Salome's blasphemous dancing. Certainly the rigid guardians of morality always look askance on the contact of the sexes in the ballroom. To be sure, the standards are relative. What appeared to one period the climax of immorality may be considered quite natural and harmless in another. In earlier centuries it was quite usual in the best society for the young man to invite the girl to a dance by a kiss, and in some times it was the polite thing for the gentleman after the dance to sit in the lap of the girl. The shifting of opinion comes to most striking expression, if we compare our present day acquiescence to the waltz with the moral indignation of our great-grandmothers. No accusers of the tango today can find more heated words against this Argentine importation than the conservatives of a hundred years ago chose in their hatred of the waltz. Good society had confined its dancing to those forms of contact in which only the hands touched each other, leaving to the peasants the [280] crude, rustic forms, and now suddenly every mother has to see her daughter clasped about the waist by any strange man. Even the dancing masters cried out against the intruder and claimed that it was illogical for a man to be allowed to press a girl to his bosom at the sound of music, while no one would dare to do it between the dances.

Thus the immorality of our most recent dances may be hardly worse than the dancing surprises of earlier fashions, but who will doubt that these sensual elements of the new social gayeties are to-day especially dangerous? The whole American atmosphere is filled with erotic thought to a degree which has been unknown throughout the history of the republic. The newspapers are filled with intra- and extra-matrimonial scandals, the playhouses commercialize the sexual instinct in lurid melodramas, sex problems are the centre of public discussion, all the old barriers which the traditional policy of silence had erected are being broken down, the whole nation is gossiping about erotics. In such inflammable surroundings where the sparks of the dance are recklessly kindled, the danger is imminent. If a nation focuses its attention on sensuality, its virile energy must naturally suffer. There is a well-known antagonism between sex and sport. [281] Perhaps the very best which may be said about sport is that it keeps boyhood away from the swamps of sexuality. The dance keeps boyhood away from the martial field of athletics.

The dance has still another psychological effect which must not be disregarded from a social point of view. It awakes to an unusual degree the impulse to imitation. The seeing of rhythmic movements starts similar motor impulses in the mind of the onlooker. It is well known that from the eleventh to the sixteenth century Europe suffered from dancing epidemics. They started from pathological cases of St. Vitus' dance and released in the excitable crowds cramplike impulses to imitative movements. But we hear the same story of instinctive imitations on occasions of less tragic character. It is reported that in the eighteenth century papal Rome was indignant over the passionate Spanish fandango. It was decided solemnly to put this wild dance under the ban. The lights of the church were assembled for the formal judgment, when it was proposed to call a pair of Spanish dancers in order that every one of the priests might form his own idea of the unholy dance. But history tells that the effect was an unexpected one. After a short time of fandango demonstration the high clerics began involuntarily to imitate the movements, and [282] the more passionately the Spaniards indulged in their native whirl, the more the whole court was transformed into one great dancing party. Even the Italian tarantella probably began as a disease with nervous dancing movements, and then spread over the land through mere imitation which led to an ecstatic turning around and around. Whoever studies the adventures of American dancing during the last season from New York to San Francisco must be impressed by this contagious character of our dancing habits. But this means that the movement carries in itself the energy to spread farther and farther, and to fill the daily life with increased longing for the ragtime. We are already accustomed to the dance at the afternoon tea; how long will it take before we are threatened by the dance at the breakfast coffee?

We have spoken of three mental effects: the license, the eroticism, and the imitativeness which are stirred up by the dancing movements. But in the perspective of history we ought not to overlook another significant trait: the overemphasis on dancing has usually characterized a period of political reaction, of indifference to public life, of social stagnation and carelessness. When the volcanoes were rumbling, the masses were always dancing. At all times when tyrants [283] wanted to divert the attention of the crowd, they gave the dances to their people. A nation which dances cannot think, but lives from hour to hour. The less political maturity, the more happiness does a national community show in its dancing pleasures. The Spaniards and the Polish, the Hungarians and the Bohemians, have always been the great dancers—the Gypsies dance. There is no fear that the New Yorkers will suddenly stop reading their newspapers and voting at the primaries; they will not become Spaniards. But an element of this psychological effect of carelessness and recklessness and stagnation may influence them after all, and may shade the papers which they read, and even the primaries at which they do vote.

Yet how one-sided would it be, if we gave attention only to the dangers which the dance may bring to a nation's mind. The credit account of the social dance is certainly not insignificant, and perhaps momentous just for the Americans of to-day. The dance is a wonderful discharge of stirred up energy; its rhythmic form relieves the tension of the motor apparatus and produces a feeling of personal comfort. The power to do this is a valuable asset, when so much emotional poverty is around us. The dance makes life smooth in the midst of hardship and drudgery. [284] For the dancer the cup is always overflowing, even though it may be small. There is an element of relaxation and of joyfulness in the rhythm of the music and the twinkling of the feet, which comes as a blessing into the dulness and monotony of life. The overworked factory girl does not seek rest for her muscles after the day of labour, but craves to go on contrasting them in the rhythmic movements of the dance. So it has been at all times. The hardest worked part of the community has usually been the most devoted to the gayety of popular dances. The refined society has in many periods of civilization declined to indulge in dancing, because it was too widely spread among the lowest working classes in towns and in the country. The dance through thousands of years has been the bearer of harmless happiness: who would refuse a welcome to such a benefactor? And with the joyfulness comes the sociability. The dance brings people near together. It is unfair to claim that the dance is aristocratic, because it presupposes leisure and luxury. On the contrary, throughout the history of civilization the dance has been above all, democratic, and has reënforced the feeling of good fellowship, of community, of intimacy, of unity. Like the popular games which melt all social groups together by a common joyful [285] interest, and like humour which breaks all social barriers, the love for dancing removes mutual distrust and harmonizes the masses.

This social effect has manifold relation to another aspect of the dance, which is psychologically perhaps the deepest: the dance is an art, and as such, of deep æsthetic influence on the whole mental life. Whenever the joy in dancing comes into the foreground, this art is developed to high artificiality. No step and no movement is left to the chance inspiration of the moment; everything is prescribed, and to learn the dances not seldom means an almost scientific study. In the great dancing periods of the rococo time the mastery of the exact rules appeared one of the most difficult parts of higher education, and as a real test of the truly cultivated gentleman and gentlewoman; scholarly books analysed every detail of the necessary forms, and the society dances in the castles of the eighteenth century were more elaborate than the best prepared ballets on the stage of to-day. But the popular dances of the really dancing nations are no less bound by traditions, and we know that even the dances of the savages are moving on in strictly inherited forms. Far from the license of haphazard movements, the self-expression of the dancer is thus regulated and bound by rules which [286] are taken by him as prescriptions of beauty. To dance thus means a steady adjustment to artistic requirements; it is an æsthetic education by which the whole system of human impulses becomes harmonized and unified. The chance movements are blended into a beautiful whole, and this reflects on the entire inner setting. Educators have for a long time been aware that calisthenics, with its subtly tuned movements of the body, develops refinement in the interplay of mental life. The personality who understands how to live in gentle, beautiful motions through that trains his mind to beauty. In Europe, for instance in Hellerau near Dresden, they have recently begun to establish schools for young men and women in which the main, higher education is to be moulded by the æsthetics of bodily expression, and the culture of the symbolic dance.

This æsthetic character of the dance, however, leads still further. It is not only the training in beautiful expression; it is the development of an attitude which is detached from practical effects and from the practical life of outer success. The dance is an action by which nothing is produced and nothing in the surroundings changed. It is an oasis in the desert of our materialistic behaviour. From morning till night we [287] are striving to do things, to manufacture something in the mill of the nation: but he who dances is satisfied in expressing himself. He becomes detached from the cares of the hour, he acquires a new habit of disinterested attitude toward life. Who can underestimate the value of such detachment in our American life? The Americans have always been eagerly at work, but have never quite learned to enjoy themselves and to take the æsthetic attitude which creates the wonders of beauty and the true harmonies of life. To forget drudgery and to sink into the rhythms of the dance may bring to millions that inner completeness which is possible only when practical and æsthetic attitude are blending in a personality. The one means restless change; the other means repose, perfection, eternity. This hardworking, pioneer nation needs the noisy teachings of efficiency and scientific management less than the [288] melodious teaching of song and dance and beauty. In short, the dance may bring both treacherous perils and wonderful gifts to our community. It depends upon us whether we reënforce the dangerous elements [289] of the dance, or the beneficial ones. It will depend on ourselves whether the dance will debase the nation, as it has so often done in the history of civilization, or whether it will help to lead it to new heights of beauty and harmony, as it has not seldom done before. Our social conscience must be wide awake; it will not [290] be a blind fate which will decide when the door of the future opens whether we shall meet the lady or the tiger.

X [291]
NAÏVE PSYCHOLOGY

The scientific psychologists started on a new road yesterday. For a long time their chief interest was to study the laws of the mind. The final goal was a textbook which would contain a system of laws to which every human mind is subjected. But in recent times a change has set in. The trend of much of the best work nowadays is toward the study of individual differences. The insight into individual personalities was indeed curiously neglected in modern psychology. This does not mean that the declaration of psychological independence insisted that all men are born equal, nor did any psychologist fancy that education or social surroundings could form all men in equal moulds. But as scientists they felt no particular interest in the richness of colours and tints. They intentionally neglected the question of how men differ, because they were absorbed by the study of the underlying laws which must hold for every one. It is hardly surprising that the [292] psychologists chose this somewhat barren way; it was a kind of reaction against the fantastic flights of the psychology of olden times. Speculations about the soul had served for centuries. Metaphysics had reigned and the observation of the real facts of life and experience had been disregarded. When the new time came in which the psychologists were fascinated by the spirit of scientific method and exact study of actual facts, the safest way was for them to imitate the well-tested and triumphant procedures of natural science. The physicist and the chemist seek the laws of the physical universe, and the psychologist tried to act like them, to study the elements from which the psychical universe is composed and to find the laws which control them. But while it was wise to make the first forward march in this one direction, the psychologist finally had to acknowledge that a no less important interest must push him on an opposite way. The human mind is not important to us only as a type. Every social aim reminds us that we must understand the individual personality. If we deal with children in the classroom or with criminals in the courtroom, with customers in the market or with patients in the hospital, we need not only to know what is true of every human being; we must above all discover how the particular [293] individual is disposed and composed, or what is characteristic of special groups, nations, races, sexes, and ages. It is clear that new methods were needed to approach these younger problems of scientific psychology, but the scientists have eagerly turned with concerted efforts toward this unexplored region and have devoted the methods of test experiments, of statistics, and of laboratory measurements to the examination of such differences between various individuals and groups.

But in all these new efforts the psychologist meets a certain public resistance, or at least a certain disregard, which he is not accustomed to find in his routine endeavours. As long as he was simply studying the laws of the mind, he enjoyed the approval of the wider public. His work was appreciated as is that of the biologist and the chemist. But when it becomes his aim to discover mental features of the individual, and to foresee what he can expect from the social groups of men, every layman tells him condescendingly that it is a superfluous task, as instinct and intuition and the naïve psychology of the street will be more successful than any measurements with chronoscopes and kymographs. Do we not know how the skilful politician or the efficient manager looks through the mind of a man [294] at the first glance? The life insurance agent has hardly entered the door before he knows how this particular mind must be handled. Every commercial traveller knows more than any psychologist can tell him, and even the waiter in the restaurant foresees when the guest sits down how large a tip he can expect from him. In itself it would hardly be convincing to claim that scientific efforts to bring a process down to exact principles are unnecessary because the process can be performed by instinct. We all can walk without needing a knowledge of the muscles which are used, and can find nourishment without knowing the physiology of nutrition. Yet the physiologist has not only brought to light the principles according to which we actually eat, but he has been able to make significant suggestions for improved diet, and in not a few cases his knowledge can render services which no instinctive appetite could replace. The psychological study of human traits, too, may not only find out the principles underlying the ordinary knowledge of men, but may discover means for an insight which goes as far beyond the instinctive understanding of man as the scientific diet prescribed by a physician goes beyond the fancies of a cook. The manager may believe that he can recognize at the first glance for which kind of work the labourer is fit: and [295] yet the psychological analysis with the methods of exact experiments may easily demonstrate that his judgment is entirely mistaken. Moreover, although such practical psychologists of the street or of the office may develop a certain art of recognizing particular features in the individual, they cannot formulate the laws and cannot lay down those permanent relations from which others may learn.

Yet even this claim of the psychological scholar seems idle pride. Had the world really to wait for his exact statistics and his formulæ of correlation of mental traits in order to get general statements and definite descriptions of the human types and of the mental diversities? Are not the writings of the wise men of all times full of such psychological observations? Has not the consciousness of the nations expressed itself in an abundance of sayings and songs, of proverbs and philosophic words, which contains this naïve psychological insight into the characters and temperaments of the human mind? We may go back thousands of years to the contemplations of oriental wisdom, we may read the poets of classic antiquity, or Shakespeare, or Goethe, we may study what the great religious leaders and statesmen, the historians and the jurists, have said about man and his behaviour; and we find an over-abundance [296] of wonderful sayings with which no textbooks of psychology can be compared.

This is all true. And yet, is it not perhaps all entirely false? Can this naïve psychology of the ages, to which the impressionism and the wisdom of the finest minds have so amply contributed, really make superfluous the scientific efforts for the psychology of groups and correlations and individual traits? It seems almost surprising that this overwhelmingly rich harvest of prescientific psychology has never been examined from the standpoint of scientific psychology, and that no one has sifted the wheat from the chaff. The very best would be not only to gather such material, but to combine the sayings of the naïve psychologists in a rounded system of psychology. In all ages they surely must have been among the best observers of mankind, as even what is not connected with the name of an individual author, but is found in proverbs or in the folk-epics of the nations, must have originated in the minds of individual leaders. My aim here is more modest: I have made my little pilgrimage through literature to find out in a tentative fashion whether the supply of psychology, outside of science, is really so rich and valuable as is usually believed. What I wish to offer, therefore, is only a first collection of psychological [297] statements, which the prescientific psychologists have proclaimed, and surely will go on proclaiming, and ought to go on proclaiming, as they do it so beautifully, where we scientists have nothing but tiresome formulæ.

Let us begin at the beginning. There has never been a nation whose contemplation was richer in wisdom, whose view of man was subtler and more suggestive, than those of old India. The sayings of its philosophers and poets and thinkers have often been gathered in large volumes of aphorisms. How many of these fine-cut remarks about man contain real psychology? The largest collection which I could discover is that of Boehtlinck, who translated seventy-five hundred Indian sayings into German. Not a few of them refer to things of the outer world, but by far the largest part of them speaks of man and of man's feeling and doing. But here in India came my first disappointment, a disappointment which repeated itself in every corner of the globe. After carefully going through those thousands of general remarks, I could not find more than a hundred and nine in which the observation takes a psychological turn. All those other thousands of reflections on men are either metaphors and comparisons of distinctly æsthetic intent, or rules of practical behaviour with social or moral or religious purpose. [298] Yet even if we turn to this 1½ per cent. which has a psychological flavour, we soon discover that among those hundred and nine, more than a half are simply definitions of the type of this: "Foolish are they who trust women or good luck, as both like a young serpent creep hither and thither," or this: "Men who are rich are like those who are drunk; in walking they are helped by others, they stagger on smooth roads and talk confusedly." It cannot be said that any psychological observations of the fool's or of the rich man's mind are recorded here. If I sift those maxims more carefully, I cannot find more than two score which, stripped of their picturesque phrasing, could really enter into that world system of naïve psychology. And yet even this figure is still too high. Of those forty, most are after all epigrams, generalizations of some chance cases, exaggerations of a bit of truth, or expressions of a mood of anger, of love, of class spirit, or of male haughtiness. The analysis of woman's mind is typical. "Inclination to lies, falsehood, foolishness, greediness, hastiness, uncleanliness, and cruelty are inborn faults of the woman"; or "Water never remains in an unbaked vessel, flour in a sieve, nor news in the mind of women"; or "The mind of a woman is less stable than the ear of an elephant or the [299] flash of lightning." On the other hand we read: "True women have twice as much love, four times as much endurance, and eight times as much modesty as men"; or "The appetite of women is twice as large, their understanding four times as large, their spirit of enterprise six times as large, and their longing for love eight times as large as that of men." Again we read: "The character of women is as changeable as a wave of the sea; their affection, like the rosy tint of a cloud in the evening sky, lasts just for a moment"; or "When women have a man's money, they let him go, as he is no longer of any use to them."

The same one-sidedness and epigrammatic exaggeration can always be felt where whole groups of men are to be characterized. "The faults of the dwarf are sixty, of the red-haired man eighty, of the humpback a hundred, and of the one-eyed man innumerable."

But let us rather turn to sayings in which the subtlety of psychological observation deserves admiration: "The drunkard, the careless, the insane, the fatigued, the angry, the hungry, the greedy, the timid, the hasty, and the lover know no law"; "If a man commits a crime, his voice and the colour of his face become changed, his look becomes furtive, and the fire is gone from his eye"; "The best remedy for a pain is no longer [300] to think of it; if you think of it, the pain will increase"; "A greedy man can be won by money, an angry man by folding the hands, a fool by doing his will, and an educated man by speaking the truth"; "The wise man can recognize the inner thoughts of another from the colour of his face, from his look, from the sound of his words, from his walk, from the reflections in his eyes, and from the form of his mouth"; "The good and bad thoughts, however much they are hidden, can be discovered from a man when he talks in his sleep or in his drunkenness"; "The ignorant can be satisfied easily, and still more easily the well educated, but a man who has become confused by a little knowledge cannot be won over even by Brahma"; "Good people are pacified by fair treatment, even if they have been very angry, but not common people; gold, though it is hard, can be melted, but not grass"; "By too great familiarity we produce low esteem, by too frequent visits, indifference; in the Malaja mountains a beggar woman uses the sandalwood tree for firewood"; "The silly man steps in without being invited, talks much without being questioned, and trusts him who does not deserve confidence"; "New knowledge does not last in the mind of the uneducated any more than a string of pearls about the neck of a monkey"; "The inner power of great men [301] becomes more evident in their misfortune than in their fortune; the fine perfume of aloes wood is strongest when it falls into the fire"; "The anger of the best man lasts an instant, of the mediocre man six hours, of the common man a day and a night, and the rascal will never get rid of it"; "The scholar laughs with his eyes, mediocre people show their teeth when they laugh, common people roar, and true men of wisdom never laugh"; "Truthfulness and cleverness can be found out in the course of a conversation, but modesty and restraint are visible at the first glance"; "Grief destroys wisdom, grief destroys scholarship, grief destroys endurance; there is no perturbation of the mind like grief." Often we hardly know whether a psychological observation or a metaphor is given to us. In any case we may appreciate the fineness of a saying like this: "Even a most translucent, beautiful, perfectly round and charming pearl can be strung on a thread as soon as it has been pierced; so a mind which longs for salvation, perfectly pure, free from quarrel with any one and full of goodness, will nevertheless be bound down to the earthly life as soon as it quarrels with itself." On the borderland of psychology we may find sayings like these: "As a tailor's needle fastens the thread in the garment, so the thread of our earthly life becomes fastened [302] by the needle of our desires"; "An elephant kills us if he touches us, a snake even if he smells us, a prince even if he smiles on us, and a scoundrel even if he adores us." But there is one saying which the most modern psychologist would accept, as it might just as well be a quotation from a report of the latest exact statistics. The Indian maxim says: "There is truth in the claim that the minds of the sons resemble more the minds of the fathers, those of the daughters more those of the mothers."

We may leave the banks of the Ganges and listen to the wisdom of Europe. Antiquity readily trusted the wonderful knowledge of men which Homer displays. He has instinctively delineated the characters with the inner truth of life. How far was this art of the creative poet accompanied by the power of psychological abstraction? I do not think that we can find in the forty-eight books of Homer even a dozen contributions to our unwritten system of the naïve psychology of the nations. To be sure we ought not to omit in such a system the following reflections from the "Odyssey": "Wine leads to folly, making even the wise to love immoderately, to dance, and to utter what had better have been kept silent"; or "Too much rest itself becomes a pain"; or still better, "The steel blade itself [303] often incites to deeds of violence." We may have more doubt whether it is psychologically true when we read: "Few sons are equal to their sires, most of them are less worthy, only a few are superior to their fathers"; or, "Though thou lovest thy wife, tell not everything which thou knowest to her, but unfold some trifle while thou concealest the rest." From the "Iliad" we may quote: "Thou knowest the over-eager vehemence of youth, quick in temper, but weak in judgment"; or, "Noblest minds are easiest bent"; or, "With everything man is satiated—sleep, sweet singing, and the joyous dance; of all these man gets sooner tired than of war." Some may even doubt whether Homer's psychology is right when he claims: "Even though a man by himself may discover the best course, yet his judgment is slower and his resolution less firm than when two go together." And in the alcohol question he leaves us a choice: "Wine gives much strength to wearied men"; or if we prefer, "Bring me no luscious wines, lest they unnerve my limbs and make me lose my wonted powers and strength."

It is not surprising that the theoretical psychology of the Bible is no less meagre. Almost every word which deals with man's mind reflects the moral and religious values and is thus removed from pure psychology into [304] ethics. Or we find comparisons which suggestively illuminate the working of the mind without amplifying our psychological understanding. We approach empirical psychology most nearly in verses like these: "Foolishness is bound in the heart of the child, but the word of correction should drive it far from him"; or "He that is faithful in that which is least, is faithful also in much; and he that is unjust in the least, is unjust also in much"; or "Stolen waters are sweet, and bread eaten in secret is pleasant"; or "The full soul loatheth an honeycomb, but to the hungry soul every bitter thing is sweet"; or "For if any man be a hearer of the word and not a doer, he is like a man beholding his natural face in a glass, for he beholdeth himself and goeth his way and straightway forgetteth what manner of man he was"; or "Sorrow is better than laughter, for by the sadness of the countenance the heart is made better." But here we have almost overstepped the limits of real psychology; we are moving toward ethics. Nor can we call metaphors like this psychology: "He that hath no rule over his own spirit is like a city that is broken down and without walls."

Let us turn for a moment to the greatest knower of men in mediæval days, to Dante. How deeply his poetic eye looked into the hearts of men, how living [305] are the characters in his "Divine Comedy"; and yet he left us hardly any psychological observations. Some psychology may be acknowledged in words like these: "The man in whose bosom thought on thought awakes is always disappointed in his object, for the strength of the one weakens the other"; "When we are wholly absorbed by feelings of delight or of grief, our soul yields itself to this one object, and we are no longer able to direct our thoughts elsewhere"; "There is no greater grief than to remember our happy time in misery." It is hardly psychology if we hear, "The bad workman finds fault with his tools"; or, "Likeness ever gives birth to love"; or "The wisest are the most annoyed to lose time."

From Dante we naturally turn to Shakespeare. We have so often heard that he is the greatest psychologist, and yet we ought not to forget that such a popular classification does not in itself really mean that Shakespeare undertakes the work of the psychologist. It does mean that he creates figures with the temperament, character, thought, and will so similar to life and so full of inner mental truth that the psychologist might take the persons of the poet's imagination as material for his psychological studies. But this by no means suggests that Shakespeare phrased abstract judgments about [306] mental life; and as we seek his wisdom in his dramatic plays, it may be taken for granted that in this technical sense he must be a poor psychologist, because he is a great dramatist. Does not the drama demand that every word spoken be spoken not from the author's standpoint, but from the particular angle of the person in the play? And this means that every word is embedded in the individual mood and emotion, thought, and sentiment of the speaker. A truly psychological statement must be general and cannot be one thing for Hamlet and another for Ophelia. The dramatist's psychological sayings serve his art, unfolding before us the psychological individuality of the speaker, but they do not contribute to the textbooks of psychology, which ought to be independent of personal standpoints. And yet what a stream of verses flows down to us, which have the ring of true psychology! "Smooth runs the water where the brook is deep."

"Trifles light as air
Are to the jealous confirmation strong
As proofs of holy writ."

"Lovers and madmen have such seething brains,
Such sharp fantasies, that apprehend
More than cool reason ever comprehends.[307] "

"Thus conscience does make cowards of us all."

"Present fears
Are less than horrible imagining."

"Too swift runs as tardy as too slow."

"Never anger made good guard for itself."

"Anger is like
A full-hot horse; who being allow'd his way
Self-mettle tires him."

"Suspicion always haunts the guilty mind."

"All things that are,

Are with more spirit chased than enjoy'd."
"Celerity is never more admir'd
Than by the negligent."
"Strong reasons make strong actions."
"The whiteness in thy cheek
Is apter than thy tongue to tell thy errand."
"The man that hath no music in himself,
Nor is not mov'd with concord of sweet sounds,
Is fit for treasons, stratagems, and spoils."
"Sweet love, I see, changing his property,[308]
Turns to the sourest and most deadly hate."
"Love is a smoke rais'd with the fume of sighs."
"I do not know the man I should avoid
So soon as that spare Cassius; he reads much;
He is a great observer."
And so on.

We all know it, and we know it so well and feel so much with Cæsar or with Lear or with Othello or with Macbeth, that we instinctively take it all for true psychology, while it after all covers just the exceptional cases of the dramatic situation.

No! If we are to seek real generalities, we must not consult the playwright. Perhaps we may find the best conditions for general statement where we do not even have to deal with an individual, but can listen to the mind of the race and can absorb its wisdom from its proverbs. Let us take the word proverb in its widest sense, including popular sayings which have not really the stamp of the proverb. There is surely no lack of sharply coined psychology. This is true of all countries. I find the harvest richest in the field of the German proverbs, but almost as many in the field of the English, and a large number of sayings are common to [309] the two countries. Very characteristic psychological remarks can be found among the Russian proverbs, and not a few among those in Yiddish. But this type of psychology is sufficiently characterized, if we confine ourselves here to the English proverbial phrases. Often they need a commentary in order to be understood in their psychological truth. We hear in almost all countries: "Children and fools speak the truth." As a matter of course we all know that their chance of speaking the objective truth is very small. What is psychologically tenable is only that they are unable to hide the subjective truth. Many such phrases are simply epigrams where the pleasure in the play of words must be a substitute for the psychological truth; for instance: "Long hair and short wit." Not a few contradict one another, and yet there is not a little wisdom in sayings like these: "Beware of a silent dog and still water"; "Misery loves company"; "Hasty love is soon hot and soon cold"; "Dogs that put up many hares kill none"; "He that will steal an egg will steal an ox"; "Idle folks have the least leisure"; "Maids say no and take"; "A boaster and a liar are cousins german"; "A young twig is easier twisted than an old tree"; "Imitation is the sincerest flattery"; "Pride joined with many virtues chokes them all"; [310] "Offenders never pardon"; "The more wit, the less courage"; "We are more mindful of injuries than of benefits"; "Where there's a will, there's a way"; "An idle brain is the devil's workshop"; "Anger and haste hinder good counsel"; "Wise men change their minds, fools never"; "Sudden joy kills sooner than excessive grief"; "Lazy folks take the most pains"; "Nature passes nurture"; "Necessity is the mother of invention"; "We are apt to believe what we wish for"; "Where your will is ready, your foot is light."

All these proverbs and the maxims of other nations may be true, but can we deny that they are on the whole so trivial that a psychologist would rather hesitate to proclaim them as parts of his scientific results? As far as they are true they are vague and hardly worth mentioning, and where they are definite and remarkable they are hardly true. We shall after all have to consult the individual authors to gather the subtler observations on man's behaviour, even though they furnish only semi-naïve psychology. But the English contributions are so familiar to every reader that it may be more interesting to listen to the foreigners. Every nation has its thinkers who have the reputation of being especially fine knowers of men. The French turn most readily to La Rochefoucauld, and the Germans [311] to Lichtenberg. Certainly a word of La Rochefoucauld beside the psychologizing proverb looks like the scintillating, well-cut diamond beside a moonstone. "We imitate good actions through emulation, and bad ones through a malignity in our nature which shame concealed and example sets at liberty"; "It is much easier to suppress a first desire than to satisfy those that follow"; "While the heart is still agitated by the remains of a passion, it is more susceptible to a new one than when entirely at rest"; "Women in love more easily forgive great indiscretions than small infidelities"; "The reason we are not often wholly possessed by a single vice is that we are distracted by several." But is this not ultimately some degrees too witty to be true, and has our system of prescientific psychology the right to open the door to such glittering epigrams which are uttered simply to tickle or to whip the vanity of man? Or what psychologist would believe Lichtenberg when he claims: "All men are equal in their mental aptitudes, and only their surroundings are responsible for their differences"? He observes better when he says: "An insolent man can look modest when he will, but a modest man can never make himself look insolent"; or when he remarks: "Nothing makes a man old more quickly than the thought that he is growing [312] older"; or "Men do not think so differently about life as they talk about it"; or "I have always found that intense ambition and suspicion go together"; or "I am convinced that we not only love ourselves in loving others, but that we also hate ourselves in hating others." Often his captivating psychological words are spoiled by an ethical trend. For instance, he has hardly the right to say: "In the character of every man is something which cannot be broken; it is the skeleton of his character." But he balances such psychological rashness by fine observations like these: "The character of a man can be recognized by nothing more surely than by the joke he takes amiss"; and "I believe that we get pale from fright also in darkness, but I do not think that we would turn red from shame in the dark, because we are pale on our own account, but we blush on account of others as well as on account of ourselves." And we are in the midst of the up-to-date psychology when we read what he said a hundred years ago: "From the dreams of a man, if he report them accurately enough, we might trace much of his character, but one single dream is not sufficient; we must have a large number for that."

I add a few characteristic words of distinctly psychological temper from the great nonpsychological authors [313] of modern times. Lessing says: "The superstition in which we have grown up does not lose its power over us when we see through it; not all who laugh about their chains are free"; or again, "We are soon indifferent to the good and even to the best, when it becomes regular"; "The genius loves simplicity, while the wit prefers complexity"; "The characteristic of a great man is that he treats the small things as small, and the important things as important"; "Whoever loses his mind from love would have lost it sooner or later in any case." But on the whole, Lessing was too much of a fighter to be truly an objective psychologist. We may put more confidence in Goethe's psychology: "Where the interest fades away, the memory soon fails, too"; "The history of man is his character"; "From nature we have no fault which may not become a virtue, and no virtue which may not become a fault"; "A quiet, serious woman feels uncomfortable with a jolly man, but not a serious man with a jolly woman"; "Whatever we feel too intensely, we cannot feel very long"; "It is easy to be obedient to a master who convinces when he commands"; "Nobody can wander beneath palms without punishment; all the sentiments must change in a land where elephants and tigers are at home"; "A man does not become [314] really happy until his absolute longing has determined its own limits"; "Hate is an active displeasure, envy a passive one, and it is therefore not surprising that envy so easily turns into hate"; "No one can produce anything important unless he isolate himself"; "However we may strive for the general, we always remain individuals whose nature necessarily excludes certain characteristics, while it possesses certain others"; "The only help against the great merits of another is love"; "Man longs for freedom, woman for tradition"; "A talent forms itself in solitude, a character in the stream of the world"; "The miracle is the dearest child of belief"; "It is not difficult to be brilliant if one has no respect for anything."

Whoever falls into the habit of looking for psychologizing maxims in his daily reading will easily bring home something which he picks up in strolling through the gardens of literature. Only we must always be on our guard lest the beautifully coloured and fragrant flowers which we pluck are poisonous. Is it really good psychology when Vauvenargues writes: "All men are born sincere and die impostors," or, when Brillat-Savarin insists: "Tell me what you eat, and I shall tell you who you are"? Or can we really trust Mirabeau: "Kill your conscience, as it is the most [315] savage enemy of every one who wants success"; or Klopstock: "Happiness is only in the mind of one who neither fears nor hopes"; or Gellert: "He who loves one vice, loves all the vices"? Can we believe Chamfort: "Ambition more easily takes hold of small souls than great ones, just as a fire catches the straw roof of the huts more easily than the palaces"; or Pascal: "In a great soul, everything is great"; or the poet Bodenstedt when he sings: "A gray eye is a sly eye, a brown eye is roguish and capricious, but a blue eye shows loyalty"? And too often we must be satisfied with opposites. Lessing tells us: "All great men are modest"; Goethe: "Only rascals are modest." The psychology of modesty is probably more neatly expressed in the saying of Jean Paul: "Modest is he who remains modest, not when he is praised, but when he is blamed": and Ebner-Eschenbach adds: "Modesty which comes to consciousness, comes to an end."

But in our system of naïve psychology, we ought not to omit such distinctly true remarks as Rabelais' much-quoted words: "The appetite comes during the eating"; or Fox's words: "Example will avail ten times more than precept"; or Moltke's: "Uncertainty in commanding produces uncertainty in obedience"; or [316] Luther's: "Nothing is forgotten more slowly than an insult, and nothing more quickly than a benefaction." It is Fichte who first said: "Education is based on the self-activity of the mind." Napoleon coins the good metaphor: "A mind without memory is a fortress without garrison." Buffon said what professional psychologists have repeated after him: "Genius is nothing but an especial talent for patience." Schumann claims: "The talent works, the genius creates." We may quote from Jean Paul: "Nobody in the world, not even women and princes, is so easily deceived as our own conscience"; or from Pascal: "Habit is a second nature which destroys the original one." Nietzsche says: "Many do not find their heart until they have lost their head"; Voltaire: "The secret of ennui is to have said everything"; Jean Paul: "Sorrows are like the clouds in a thunderstorm; they look black in the distance, but over us hardly gray." Once more I quote Nietzsche: "The same emotions are different in their rhythm for man and woman: therefore men and women never cease to misunderstand each other."

This leads us to the one topic to which perhaps more naïve psychology has been devoted than to any other psychological problem, the mental difference between [317] men and women. Volumes could be filled, and I think volumes have been filled, with quotations about this eternal source of happiness and grief. But if we look into those hundreds of thousands of crisp sayings and wise maxims, we find in the material of modern times just what we recognized in the wisdom of India. Almost all is metaphor and comparison, or is practical advice and warning, or is enthusiastic praise, or is maliciousness, but among a hundred hardly one contains psychology. And if we really bring together such psychologizing observations, we should hardly dare to acknowledge that they deserve that right of generality by merit of which they might be welcomed to our psychological system. Bruyere insists: "Women are extreme; they are better or worse than men"; and the same idea is formulated by Kotzebue: "When women are good they stand between men and angels; when they are bad, they stand between men and devils." Rousseau remarks: "Woman has more esprit, and man more genius; the woman observes, and the man reasons." Jean Paul expresses the contrast in this way: "No woman can love her child and the four quarters of the globe at the same time, but a man can do it." Grabbe thinks: "Man looks widely, woman deeply; for man the world is the heart, for woman the heart [318] is the world." Schiller claims: "Women constantly return to their first word, even if reason has spoken for hours." Karl Julius Weber, to whom German literature has to credit not a few psychological observations, says: "Women are greater in misfortune than men on account of the chief female virtue, patience, but they are smaller in good fortune than men, on account of the chief female fault, vanity." Yet as to patience, a German writer of the seventeenth century, Christoph Lehmann, says: "Obedience and patience do not like to grow in the garden of the women." But I am anxious to close with a more polite German observation. Seume holds: "I cannot decide whether the women have as much reason as the men, but I am perfectly sure that they have not so much unreason." And yet: "How hard it is for women to keep counsel," and how many writers since Shakespeare have said this in their own words.

The poets, to be sure, feel certain that in spite of all these inner contradictions, they know better than the psychologists, and where their knowledge falls short, they at least assure the psychologist that he could not do better. Paul Heyse, in his booklet of epigrammatic stanzas, writes a neat verse which, in clumsy prose, says: "Whoever studies the secrets of the soul may [319] bring to light many a hidden treasure, but which man fits which woman no psychologist will ever discover." To be sure, as excuse for his low opinion of us psychologists, it may be said that when he wrote it in Munich thirty years ago there was no psychological laboratory in the university of his jolly town and only two or three in the world. But to-day we have more than a hundred big laboratories in all countries, and even Munich now has its share in them, so that Heyse may have improved on his opinion since then. But in any case we psychologists do not take our revenge by thinking badly of the naïve psychology of the poets and of the man on the street. Yet we have seen that their so-called psychology is made up essentially of picturesque metaphors, or of moral advice, of love and malice, and that we have to sift big volumes before we strike a bit of psychological truth; even then, how often it has shown itself haphazard and accidental, vague and distorted! The mathematical statistics of the professional students of the mind and their test experiments in the laboratories are certainly less picturesque, but they have the one advantage that the results are true. Mankind has no right to deceive itself with half-true, naïve psychology of the amateur, when our world is so full of social problems which will be solved only if [320] the aptitudes and the workings of the mind are clearly recognized and traced. The naïve psychology is sometimes stimulating and usually delightful, but if reliable psychology is wanted, it seems after all that only one way is open—to consult the psychologists.